NOTHING TO GRASP

Joan Tollifson

NON-DUALITY PRESS

NOTHING TO GRASP

First edition published August 2012 by NON-DUALITY PRESS

© Joan Tollifson 2012
© Non-Duality Press 2012

Author photo: David Lorenz Winston
Cover image: Joan Tollifson

Joan Tollifson has asserted her right under the Copyright, Designs
and Patents Act, 1988, to be identified as author of this work.

NON-DUALITY PRESS | PO Box 2228 | Salisbury | SP2 2GZ
United Kingdom

ISBN: 978-1-908664-24-2

www.non-dualitypress.org

No matter what state dawns at this moment, can there be just that? Not a movement away, an escape into something that will provide what this state does not provide, or doesn't seem to provide: energy, zest, inspiration, joy, happiness, whatever. Just completely, unconditionally listening to what's here now, is that possible?

—Toni Packer

That which is before you is it, in all its fullness, utterly complete. There is naught beside. Even if you go through all the stages of a Bodhisattva's progress toward Buddhahood, one by one; when at last, in a single flash, you attain to full realization, you will only be realizing the Buddha-Nature which has been with you all the time; and by all the foregoing stages you will have added to it nothing at all.

—Huang Po

Contents

Preface vii

Life 1

This Is It! 9

The Imaginary Problem 17

The Original Face 24

Is That All There Is? 27

What Is Looking Out of My Eyes? 29

No Self 35

Is the Body Real? Am I the Body? 43

Not Taking Your Life Personally 48

What Is This? 53

Not Making Something Out of Nothing 58

Not One, Not Two 63

What Should I Do? 67

Choice and Choicelessness 73

Awareness 86

Is There *Anything* to Do? 95

Control and Surrender 116

The Flow: Inhaling and Exhaling 123

What If We Really Are Perfect, Just As We Are? 128

The Pathless Path to Here / Now 132

The Art of Going Nowhere 139

Inquiry: What is It? 151

Turning to Face the Imaginary Tiger 156

Am I Enlightened Yet? 158

Many Ways Home 164

The Simplicity of What Is 168

Just When You Get It, It's Over! 172

Acknowledgments 175

Preface

This book is about liberation. That doesn't mean the end of earthquakes, wars, bankruptcies, unemployment and cancer, and it doesn't mean a life without heartbreak, depression, anxiety or addiction. It's about recognizing that *this* is the Holy Reality, and that the Holy Reality is not somewhere else. It's the realization that the fundamental problem can only be resolved now, and that actually, there is nothing to resolve. Liberation is finding freedom in limitation and perfection in imperfection. It is the freedom to be exactly as we are. But what *are* we? What is real Here/Now? What is life all about? Who is reading these words? Is reading these words an individual choice, or is it the only possible activity of the whole universe at this moment, and is there a difference? Is there a practice that leads to liberation, or does that very idea reinforce the illusion that there is someone who is bound and that liberation is "out there" somewhere in the future? This book explores these questions.

It doesn't aim to provide answers, but rather, to undermine the assumptions behind the questions, to expose the imaginary nature of our apparent problems and dilemmas. This book invites an open listening and looking. It is not about acquiring new beliefs, but rather, it is an invitation to discover what requires no believing in order to be.

Joan Tollifson
Southern Oregon
Early Spring, 2012

Life

Life is continually living on life. Life appears in all sorts of forms and shapes. But it is still the same life, the same intelligence-energy. And you are that life.

—Sailor Bob Adamson

The delicacy of late afternoon sunlight on a single trembling leaf, white clouds sliding through the blue sky, children being sold into prostitution, starving refugees fleeing a famine, incredible acts of generosity and kindness, the sinking ache of depression, oil spilling into the oceans. Life has so many faces—beautiful in one moment, excruciating in the next, horrific beyond comprehension, exquisite beyond words.

When it is beautiful, our only suffering is in knowing it won't last. When it is ugly, it can feel overwhelming and terrifying. Even if we don't have to personally experience or witness the most horrific things that are going on, even if we are completely ignorant of such things, we are in fact touched by all of them, for we are not really separate from the people in faraway places or from the oceans and the air we breathe. And we each have our own personal struggles with disappointment, loneliness, economic uncertainty, chronic pain, disability, addiction—whatever the particular mix is for each one of us.

How do we make sense of all this? What's it all about? Is there any way out of our suffering or the world suffering, or any way to live through it without falling into destructive mind-states like despair, anger, hatred, and self-pity?

Like many others, I looked in different directions for answers to these questions. I tried alcohol and drugs, psychotherapy, political activism, meditation, satsang and radical nonduality. Finally I arrived at the place I had never left: the simplicity and immediacy of Here / Now—*this* that is ever-present and utterly complete *in spite* of what happens in the movie of waking life and never *because* of what happens.

I still experience moments of heartbreak and discouragement, bursts of anger, waves of depression or anxiety, and periodic flare-ups of addictive and compulsive behaviors. Perhaps these things happen less frequently, less severely and for shorter duration, but they still happen. And the world at large is still full of suffering and injustice.

What does seem to have changed is that there has been a falling away of the thought-sense that I am a separate person in charge of "my life" who is going to eventually perfect myself or the world. There is the realization that life includes the whole show, the light and the dark, that none of it is personal, that all of it is happening effortlessly by itself in the only way possible, and that none of it has any solidity or permanence. There is also clarity about *what* the unnecessary exertion is that gives rise to so much of our human suffering and confusion, how we make ourselves miserable. As this has clarified, there has been a decrease in gullibility when the siren song of delusion appears. When I find myself thinking that something is lacking or that the fix is "out there" somewhere, there is a greater ability to relax into Here/Now, the place I have never really left.

Instead of trying to intentionally fix or improve "myself" or "the world," I am more open to allowing everything to heal itself in its own way, in its own time, as it does anyway. There is a devotion to the immediacy of life exactly as it is right now, without superimposing any kind of spin. This bare intimacy is neither an effortful, goal-oriented, improvement-seeking exertion, nor is it any kind of passive or fatalistic resignation. It is an energetic aliveness, an openness that includes everything and sticks to nothing. It is not something "you" achieve or acquire, but simply the boundlessness, the bare being that is always already fully present right here, right now.

It is a great relief to realize that in this undivided happening, there is no perfection apart from the imperfection, that the light and the dark arise together like the crest and trough of the wave, that they cannot be pulled apart, and to appreciate the holiness of everything, exactly as it is, warts and all. The firm conviction that I know what's best for the universe seems thankfully to be evaporating. And when it does show up, it has more of an endearing quality—oh look, there goes Joan doing her little dance of concern again.

I've discovered that there is no end to problems. When we cure one problem, a new one emerges. But this only becomes a source of suffering if we imagine it should or could be otherwise. In fact, the turbulent, cloudy weather is as integral to the whole as the clear, sunny weather. And it's all a matter of perspective and point of view what we consider sunny. Every time we take a step or scratch our nose, we are killing and maiming millions of microorganisms, but we don't give this mass killing a second thought. We regard the extermination of a virus or a bunch of cancer cells as a positive thing, and we feel no moral outrage if one ant colony invades and enslaves another ant colony. But our human drama, by contrast, seems serious and full of meaning, and our particular point of view feels very real and "right" to us.

In the movie of waking life that starts playing every morning, I seem to be a character in an unfolding drama, and whenever I turn on the news, the world seems to be an epic battleground between good and evil. The story is mesmerizing and seems very real. But then magically, every night in deep sleep, the whole movie disappears and I disappear along with it. What remains in deep sleep can never be perceived or conceived. It is the groundless ground, that which is prior to consciousness, that which *is* consciousness. In night dreams and in the dream-like movie of waking life, this groundlessness appears as infinite forms. When we look closely, we see that these forms are nothing but continuous change, and that no solid, independent persisting thing ever actually forms except conceptually, as an idea.

The whole show is one seamless, ever-changing, ungraspable happening: subatomic particles waving in and out of existence, planets circling the sun, hurricanes sweeping across the ocean, birds migrating, ants building tunnels and hills, white blood cells battling an infection, humans clear-cutting a forest, building a meditation center, writing books, shopping for groceries, driving to work, falling in love, getting angry, waking, dreaming, daydreaming, waking up from daydreaming, thinking, remembering, imagining, hearing the traffic, reading these words. Only when we *think* about this seamless flow and put it into words, does it *apparently* get broken up into subjects and objects, nouns and verbs, causes and effects, before and after, good and bad. Only when we *think*, does there *seem* to be an unfolding narrative happening in time with "me" at the center of the story, an apparently separate unit of consciousness (a mind) encapsulated inside an apparently separate body, someone who must make something of myself, use my gifts to help the world, be a success, do the right thing, and perhaps get enlightened.

But if we look backward with awareness for the source of any impulse, thought, desire, intention, action or reaction that occurs, no point of origination can be located or found. We have no idea what our next thought will be. Recent brain research indicates that by the time a thought such as, "I need to feed the cat," shows up in consciousness, the action this thought appears to initiate is in fact already underway in the body. In the blink of an eye, the forms of this moment vanish into thin air, replaced instantly by an entirely new universe. When we look closely at any apparent form (a chair, a person, a thought, a feeling, a sensation), it's obvious that none of what appears has any substantial, persisting reality. Everything is changing, dissolving into something else. It is all a shimmering, dream-like appearance, vanishing as soon as it appears.

Everything is changing, and yet paradoxically, Here / Now is ever-present.

Whatever time of day or night it appears to be, whatever year it is, however old I seem to be, whatever location is showing up, it is always happening Here / Now—there is only this timeless, placeless, ownerless eternity that never comes, never goes, and never stays the same. This aware presence, this immediacy, this seamlessness that I call Here / Now is the water in every wave. This moment, just as it is, is unavoidable and inescapable.

We typically imagine ourselves to be an enduring, independent entity with free will, a separate fragment apart from the whole, struggling to control our life and survive as this conceptual form called "me" that we think is real. We fear death and hope that "my" consciousness and my story will continue on in some kind of hopefully pleasant after-life. But this picture of our situation is as ill-conceived as the one our ancestors had not that long ago when they feared that they might fall off the edge of the earth if they sailed out into the ocean. When we truly see that there is no separate, independent, persisting form of any kind—that no actual borders or seams exist between subject and object, self and not-self, birth and death—that there is only this ever-changing, ever-present boundlessness—then there is no body and no mind apart from the totality. Just as there is no edge to the earth, there is no independent or persisting *someone* who is born and who eventually dies. There is only this inexplicable thorough-going flux or boundless presence, just as it is, from which nothing stands apart—vast emptiness flowering into this ever-changing appearance.

We are each much more (and much less) than what we have imagined ourselves to be. We are each the unnamable presence-awareness that has no center, no owner, no location, no boundary, no form, no beginning and no end. We are each the whole universe and what remains when the universe ends. And at the same time, quite undeniably, we each seem to be playing the part of a particular character, and each of us is apparently watching and acting in a completely unique movie of waking life. Like snowflakes, no two movies are exactly alike. But we might notice that this character is a kind of intermittent, ever-changing, mirage-like appearance that comes and goes, along with all the other characters and the ever-changing scenery in this dream-like movie of waking life, and that it is only *in* the movie that we seem to be a bunch of separate people with separate bodies, separate minds and separate movies.

We could say that everything is the play of consciousness, whatever "consciousness" is. The truth is, life is a mysterious event that can never really be captured by any scientific or metaphysical formulation. And yet being here now—this present happening—is undeniable, obvious and unavoidable. It is only mysterious when we try to explain it or make sense of it conceptually.

I've noticed that whenever suffering or confusion appears, it means that consciousness is lost in thought, entranced in a kind of hypnotic dream-world. It has forgotten that it is the whole ocean, and it is identifying itself as a particular wave and then trying desperately to survive as that wave, trying to be a successful wave. It is even seeking the ocean! When there is a recognition that no wave exists apart from the ocean, when there is no imaginary separation between "me" and this present happening, suffering ends. The problem vanishes, and I vanish as that imaginary somebody who seemingly needs to make something of myself and save the world and figure everything out and shift into some higher state of consciousness. There is simply this present moment, just as it is.

This waking up from the dream of separation can only happen now, not forever-after or in the future, and it isn't so much something that *happens* as it is the utter simplicity of Here / Now, just as it is. This simple, bare being is incredibly obvious and *actually* unavoidable. It *seems* elusive only because it is so close at hand, so all-inclusive.

It's not a matter of understanding all this intellectually, but rather, of recognizing what requires no understanding, what is truly inconceivable but at the same time completely obvious and totally unavoidable. It is about recognizing the nonconceptual immediacy that is right here, right now. And actually, this recognition is never not here, for nothing is not this. Even the thoughts and stories that *seem* to take us away are nothing *other* than this seamless happening—they are momentary appearances in the ever-changing kaleidoscope of Here / Now—bursts of energy with no inherent form or enduring existence. The Holy Reality is truly unavoidable, even though it can *seemingly* be obscured or overlooked. Liberation is not the attainment or acquisition of something new, and it is not the result of a cause, but rather, it is the ever-present, undivided immediacy from which nothing stands apart. Liberation is really a non-happening, a shiftless shift, or as they say in Zen, a gateless gate. It is Here / Now.

This Is It!

We habitually tend to think that "this isn't it." Identified as a separate fragment, we inevitably feel incomplete and vulnerable. We are deeply convinced that something is missing, that things are not quite right. Above all, we feel convinced that "I" am not entirely okay. We hear that "this is it" or that "everything is perfect just as it is," and we cannot believe that this could possibly be true.

We humans seem to have an intense desire for things to be different than they are. Maybe this is how we have evolved, through our urge to explore and our curiosity about what is around the bend. Desire and fear are part of our survival system, and in a biological sense, they serve us well. Our ability to identify errors and envision new possibilities has allowed us to survive and prosper. But these same abilities also seem to get us into self-defeating quandaries that no other animal faces.

We not only desire a nourishing meal and a warm place to sleep like any other animal, but we may also desire things that will kill us like cigarettes and crack cocaine. Fueled by a mix of ordinary desires and fatal attractions, humans have come up with an entire industry devoted to creating unnecessary desire and stirring up a false sense of lack, and much of the world is now dominated by an economic and political system that survives by encouraging suicidal forms of consumption, an addictive cycle that appears to be destroying the very earth upon which we depend for our survival. Crack cocaine and cigarettes are just the tip of the iceberg when it comes to the kinds of self-destructive muddles that no other animal has enough brains to conjure up. Of course, all of this is no less natural than the destructive activities of locusts, viruses, cancer cells, parasites, wild fires, hurricanes, exploding suns, ice ages or stray meteorites smashing into planets.

Although we often think of ourselves as something outside of nature or beyond nature, or perhaps as some kind of unnatural aberration; in fact, our complex brains and our human activity are as much an expression of nature as anything else. Our skyscrapers, highways and weapons of mass destruction are every bit as natural as beaver dams, ant hills and bee stings. And likewise, modern medicine, political movements fighting for social justice, spiritual practices such as meditation and books like this one are also an expression of nature, just as the white blood cells battling an infection in the body are an expression of nature. *Everything* is included in what is.

But because of our ability to engage in abstract thought and our ability to remember the past and imagine the future, we humans are always getting the idea that something is missing. We think this unsettling, gnawing sense of lack might be satiated if only we had a new car, a better job, a bigger house, a different mate, an end to arthritis, another café latte, a more just social-economic system, or a magnificent enlightenment experience. There's nothing wrong with wanting or having any of these things, but we suffer when we imagine that these things will truly resolve our fundamental unease or bring us real happiness and peace of mind. Inevitably, we are disappointed. What we most deeply desire is actually very close at hand, here and now. It is what we *are*, what we cannot *not* be: the beingness, the aliveness, the presence, the emptiness that doesn't depend on what form this moment takes, whether it is a new car or a flat tire, for the real source of true happiness, peace and freedom is equally present in every form.

What am I talking about?

This! Right here. Right now. The aliveness and immediacy of *this* present experiencing, the *knowingness* of being present and aware, this inescapable Here / Now—*this* that you always already are and cannot not be—the bare actuality of *just this,* exactly as it is.

Still not sure what I mean?

For a few minutes, after you read this paragraph, put the book down and simply be present without doing anything special. Feel the breathing. Notice the sounds of traffic, wind, birds singing, children playing, planes flying overhead, whatever you are hearing. Feel the sensations in the body. Enjoy the shapes, colors and movements that are appearing as pure visual sensation without labeling them and trying to make sense of them. Whenever you notice you are thinking, if you can, let the thoughts go and return to this simple, bare, naked experiencing of the present moment. Allow your experience to be exactly the way it is, however it is. You're not trying to get rid of anything, or accomplish anything, or understand anything. You're simply being here, which is effortless. You can't *not* be here, exactly as you are, so you don't need to *do* anything or *not* do anything. Let yourself simply *be.* Stay with this bare being for a few minutes—breathing, hearing, seeing, sensing, awaring—simply being alive. Can you sense the difference between the bare *actuality* of present moment breathing-hearing-seeing-sensing-awaring-being and any attempt to capture this happening in words, concepts or metaphysical formulations? Can you see that reality itself (bare experiencing) is at once inconceivable and utterly obvious?

Of course, thinking and conceptualizing are also a part of this seamless happening, but it is only in thinking and conceptualizing that we seem to get caught up in imaginary problems and dilemmas. It is only conceptually, in thought-generated stories, that we seem to be "somebody" who needs to be different from how we are. That's why it can be so liberating when attention shifts from thoughts to the bare simplicity of hearing, seeing, sensing, awaring.

Of course, when that shift happens, when we feel the relief of simply being here as nothing at all, thought will often pop up and try to claim this as a personal achievement: "I've got it! This is it! I'm enlightened!" And that very thought instantly recreates the mirage of "me" and "it," the mirage of separation and duality. Next thing we know, there is another thought: "Oh no! I lost it! How can I get it back?" And the great secret is that *all* of this—the thoughts, the mirage of "me," the bare sensations, the awareness that beholds it all, the whole show—all of this is without self, without separation, without substance. It is one unavoidable and thus unattainable *suchness*.

Words like "Here / Now," or statements such as "this is It," are pointing to this eternal present moment that has no location, no boundary, no seams. Here / Now is ever-present and ever-changing. It is showing up as traffic sounds, the taste of an apple, the blueness of the blue sky, the sensations of a headache, the stories and mental movies created by thought and imagination, and the no-experience of deep sleep. I'm pointing to what is most obvious, most immediate, most undeniable—the bare actuality of *what is*—this bare being that requires no belief and that is impossible to doubt.

Any *interpretation* of this present experiencing (*what* it is, or *why* it is) can be doubted, but *that* it is, is beyond doubt. You can doubt any *conclusions* you draw about this present experiencing (for example, that it's a brain creation based on sensory input from an external world made up of chemicals, atoms, molecules, subatomic particles, quarks or strings, or that it's all consciousness, or that it's a dream or an illusion)—these conclusions can all be doubted, but the bare *experiencing* of this present happening, the *here-ness* or *now-ness* or *suchness* of it, *this* requires no belief and is impossible to deny. Even if we believe it to be an illusion or a dream, it is still undeniably appearing.

Awake to this present aliveness, there is an openness and a sense of wonder. We see beauty in the most ordinary things. We sense that everything is fundamentally okay even if it apparently isn't. We feel an ease of being. Even if we are grieving or feeling physical pain, there is an aliveness to it, a sense of fluidity and groundlessness.

Asleep to this present aliveness, there is suffering. I'm distinguishing here between pain (which is bare sensation) or painful circumstances (such as war, bankruptcy, a natural disaster) and the thoughts, stories and beliefs *about* the pain or the painful circumstances. Suffering, as I'm using the word here, is basically the thought-story-belief-idea that *this-here-now* is not enough, that life *shouldn't* be the way it is, that "I" am not okay or "it" is not okay—that what we long for is "out there" somewhere, in the past or the future, someplace or sometime other than Here / Now. This idea of lack is always rooted in the underlying thought-story-belief-idea that "I" am a separate fragment encapsulated inside a perishable and vulnerable bodymind, looking out at an alien and threatening world, trying to survive and succeed and get somewhere and be somebody special. From this perspective of separation and encapsulation, something always seems to be missing.

We imagine that *someday* we can be fully alive—*after* we get our debts paid off, *after* we clean out the garage, *after* we stop smoking for good, *after* we learn Spanish, *after* we volunteer to help feed the homeless, *after* we get a job, *after* we've saved up enough for retirement, *after* we retire, *after* we lose weight, *after* we get back to the gym and get in shape again, *after* we make amends with our parents, *after* we find our soul mate and get married, *after* the children are successfully launched, *after* we go on another retreat, *after* we get enlightened—*then*, someday, in the future, we can be fully alive, fully okay. Our real life can finally begin. Or maybe we think our real life was in the past, *before* the divorce, *before* we lost our job, *before* the children left home, *before* we got cancer and ended up in a wheelchair. But either way, whether our obsession is with the past or the future, *this*, right now, can't be it. *This* is a mess. That's what we think.

To awaken is to see through these thoughts, to wake up from the story of my life and from everything I think and believe, to wake up to the simplicity of *what is*. This can only happen Here / Now, not in the past or the future. To be awake is to recognize the infinite in the finite, the emptiness in every form, the perfection in the apparent imperfection, the wholeness in multiplicity. There is nothing apart from Here / Now, and therefore, no one is ever really lost and there is to nothing to find that is not already fully present.

Try to grasp what Here / Now is, what awareness is, what presence is, and it slips through your fingers like water or air. And yet, this present happening, this aware presence, is utterly obvious and totally undeniable. It is the only "thing" that is absolutely beyond doubt (and it isn't a *thing* at all for it is nothing in particular and it is *everything*). To *seek* for this aware presence is an absurdity because there is nowhere and nothing that is outside Here / Now. Even suffering and the story of separation and lack is nothing but Here / Now appearing as that story, appearing as suffering. Without awareness, it could not appear at all. Samsara (the movie of waking life) is nirvana (the Holy Reality) in thin disguise.

Suffering is like a thunderstorm or a cloudy day. It has no owner. It doesn't *mean* anything. Although suffering *seems* personal, it is really no more personally owned or caused than the weather.

This present happening is not something "outside of you" or separate from you, anymore than this aware presence is something "inside of you," for no actual border between inside and outside can ever be found. There may be a *conceptual* boundary-line that we *think* is there, but like a line on a map between two countries, this dividing line isn't *really* there in actuality. To discover this absence of any boundary directly, simply look closely (with awareness, not with analytical thought) for the place where "inside of you" turns into "outside of you."

You may discover that there is only this undivided happening, ever-changing and full of infinite variation, but always appearing Here / Now as one seamless picture, one whole movie, in which there is no "seer" and no "seen" apart from the seeing.

The Imaginary Problem

*I have been through some terrible things in my life,
some of which actually happened.*

—Mark Twain

*Ask yourself first, "Who is it who is looking for
liberation, who finds himself in bondage?" In that
question you will find the answer. You will see there
is nothing. There is nobody.*

—Jean Klein

*We could have the biggest problem going, and I
mean the biggest neurotic obsession imaginable, and
still it is all nothing but present experience. This
understanding is completely liberating, once we get
used to it.*

—J. Matthews

Humans have long been searching for the ground of
being, the source and substance of life itself. Atoms, subatomic particles, strings, consciousness, awareness, God,
primordial energy—many possibilities have been put
forth by science, metaphysics and religion over the centuries. Whether science looks "outward" astronomically
or "inward" subatomically, it is always pushing past its

previous limits. It has even found that the act of observing changes what is being observed, that objectivity does not exist.

We wonder if the world "really is" the way we perceive it, and in countless ways, we discover that perception is unreliable, that it can be tricked. And yet we tend to overlook the obvious fact that the *suchness* of present perceiving is utterly beyond doubt. We can doubt whether the gun we thought we saw in the man's hand was really a gun or whether it was a cell phone, an optical illusion or a hallucination, but we cannot doubt the bare *suchness* of that gun-like shape, the pure perceiving itself. And, in fact, any conclusion we arrive at about what that object "really" was (or is), is always subject to doubt, perhaps because there is no separate and persisting objective reality "out there" apart from the seamlessness of present experiencing. And there is also no separate and persisting subject "in here" to be fooled.

Because we tend to pay more attention to our conceptual interpretations than to the bare actuality of being, we easily become confused and distressed. We can't understand how people on the opposite side of the political spectrum can possibly be so totally and maddeningly blind to how the world "really" is. Or we worry that the world we perceive might be a simulated reality created by hostile machines to deceive and enslave us, that we might turn out to be a brain in a vat. Or we hear that there is a split-second time-delay in perception so that we are always perceiving only the past, as if we were looking out the rear window of a car watching the landscapes disappear behind us, and this seems terribly disturbing because how can we steer the car if we can't see where we actually are, much less where we're going?

Or we agree that everything is one undivided happening, but we worry that maybe "I" am not experiencing it that way. Or we nod in agreement that everything is only a dream-like appearance and that the self is only an illusion, and then we ask, so now what should I do? These all seem like reasonable concerns if we buy into the dualistic assumptions and misconceptions underlying these apparent conundrums.

But who exactly is the one who has these concerns, the one who seems to be at the center of these disturbing scenarios, the one who imagines itself as something separate from present experiencing, the one who thinks it has to steer the car, the one who is worried about being duped? And where are *any* of these scenarios, "real" or "imagined," taking place? We can *think* or *imagine* that there is a world outside of consciousness, independent of consciousness, but that thought or imagination only happens *in* consciousness. In fact, we never experience *anything* outside of consciousness, and yet where is consciousness happening? If we cut open the brain, we won't find this room we seem to be sitting in right now, or this world, or the landscapes of our dreams and imaginations. So where exactly *is* all of this happening? If you're looking for the answer, you're already falling for the imaginary problem, and anything you find will be just another object appearing in consciousness. It is worth noting that every night in deep sleep, all these problems disappear along with the one who seems to have them.

For centuries we thought our planet, presumed to be a flat plain, was at the center of the universe. Then we discovered that the earth went around the sun and was only one of many planets in one of many solar systems in one of many galaxies in what suddenly appeared to be a godless universe where no benevolent being was in control and looking out for us. We also assumed for many centuries that we were each somebody, an executive self with free will authoring our thoughts and choosing our actions. Recent brain research has increasingly shown this picture to be every bit as absurdly false as imagining a flat earth at the center of the universe. Once again we have been thrown into metaphysical uncertainty and despair. Not only is there no god running the show, now it seems there is no "me" running the show either! Eeek!

Of course, what has *really* changed with these scientific discoveries? Only our conceptual picture, our mental image, our story about our situation, our map of reality. The new map gives rise to new stories, new imaginations and new fears, and these all seem very real.

Terrified of being nothing more than a helpless robot cursed with self-awareness adrift in a cold, meaningless, nihilistic universe full of scary black holes, we try desperately to soothe our distress. We stroke our hand-held devices, take up meditation, do yoga, rush from one satsang to the next and read endless books about non-duality, desperately seeking a solution to the imaginary problem. And although there are brief moments of happiness and satisfaction, moments when we forget about the imaginary problem, we notice that ultimately, all the solutions turn out to be disappointing. For many of us, no matter how ardently we try to believe in our latest religion, our latest guru, or our latest set of answers, there is always this niggling doubt, this persistent uncertainty, this fundamental unease. And we definitely don't want to be conned, duped, placated or fooled by false conclusions the way our ancestors were. We're perpetually on guard. Skepticism becomes our path, often alternating with gullibility and brief flings with hopeful new solutions.

If we're lucky, we may eventually notice that in any moment when we stop running from this unease, it vanishes into thin air. When we drop all our beliefs and ideas and stop searching for answers and solutions, the problem disappears.

The apparent problem only exists, or seems to exist, when there is the misconception that we are separate from our experience. All our doubt and distress refer to and revolve around the illusory sense of a separate self.

The separate self is searching for meaning and trying to figure out the truth about the universe, as if truth were something outside of present experiencing that could be figured out and as if meaning were something "out there" that could be found.

But when we relax into what is effortlessly happening all by itself Here / Now, we discover peace, freedom, love, joy—all the things we were searching for "out there."

Of course, saying this is dangerous because the reader may be tempted to examine present experience and "look for" peace, freedom, love and joy—and then evaluate whether these qualities are present or not. This very activity of standing back and examining experience, "looking for" something, immediately creates a sense of separation, unease and lack, and then thought pops up to confirm the reality of this lack and take it personally by asserting that, "I don't have the qualities that she was describing. I'm not getting it. I'm a loser. I'll probably never get it."

But the "I" who is supposedly a loser is only a mirage-like mental image that thought has just materialized out of thin air, as is the apparent lack. The entire problem is imaginary as is the one who supposedly has the problem. It does no good to believe this—then we just have a new religion that will soon become doubtful. What dissolves the imaginary problem is seeing through both the problem and the one who seems to have it whenever they show up.

And watch how quickly the mind turns even that into a new self-improvement task for the salvation of "me." My new task becomes seeing through the imaginary problem, so that "I" can arrive at a better place and become a more enlightened "me," and my new story is how well or how poorly I am doing at this. This is the same old spin again.

There *is* a natural desire to wake up, not just for the sake of our self-image, and this is the natural functioning of life: healing wounds, finding solutions, clarifying what is obscured. It is love in action. But this natural devotion is quite different from an obsession with self-improvement rooted in the very misconceptions it is trying to fix. We can *feel* the difference between the openness of love and the tightness of grasping.

But remember that the tightness, the misconceptions and the wounds are all part of life too. Nothing is left out. Unicity includes absolutely *everything*. Only the mirage-like separate fragment, the character in the movie, is concerned about being perfect and not being fooled again. The wholeness of being doesn't mind being fooled. Awareness has no self-image to protect, no self to defend against death. For life itself, there is no end to being fooled and no end to waking up. It is all happening to no one. It's not personal.

So if you find yourself obsessively thinking about conceptual problems, you might begin to notice how unsatisfying this mental spinning is, how it never really works. There is something alluring about it—it's familiar, it promises great results, it seems safer than relaxing into boundlessness—but like so many other alluring activities, it doesn't deliver. You only get more and more confused and desperate. The treadmill goes faster and faster, but the carrot doesn't get any closer. Being aware of this whole mechanism whenever it shows up begins to dissolve its credibility and its allure. Being aware doesn't mean thinking about it. It means *seeing* it as it happens. You may find that there is an ability to let the thoughts go, to come back to the simplicity of this moment, to relax into the open space of awareness. And in this open space, you may discover that no problems remain.

The Original Face

*Love is the ability to see every circumstance and
every being as perfect just as they are.*

—Anam Thubten

Can you sense the aliveness and the spaciousness of this
present happening that you are, this boundlessness that
includes the whole universe?

A truck speeding past, sunlight warming the skin,
the movement of toes and fingers, a forest fire racing
across a dry landscape, a mother in Africa cradling her
starving child, a wealthy investment banker in New York
sipping a martini, a serial killer torturing his victim, a
doctor saving a patient, soldiers in a war shooting at each
other, microorganisms battling it out in the bloodstream,
an ant running across the sidewalk, a gigantic foot crush-
ing the ant, explosions in a distant galaxy—can you
sense that all of this is one seamless movement happening
in perfect synchronicity and harmony even when there is
apparent discord and dissonance? Can you see that there
is no boundary between you (this aware presence) and
everything that appears?

The child molester, the serial killer, the drunk who
dies on the sidewalk in a pool of urine and vomit are no
less the Holy Reality than the mother who lovingly cares

for her children, the aid worker who goes to help the famished, or the monk who lives a life of pristine serenity and clarity. And at the center of everything (every form, every sensation, every perception, every idea), if we look closely, we find no-thing at all, only that which cannot be found for it is too close, too intimate to grasp.

The wonder of life is intimately connected to its transience and insubstantiality. Everything changes and no passing form has any enduring existence. Our childhood, our greatest relationship, our most embarrassing moment, the moon landing, the holocaust, the events of September 11, the stories on the nightly news, the entire history of the world, our whole life at the moment of our death—all these things pass before us and vanish like dreams (or nightmares). What is undeniable in every passing form, what cannot be doubted, is the *suchness* of it, the present-ness.

Presence (or emptiness) is not a "thing" that can be grasped. Awareness is not *something* that is "out there" separate from everything it reveals. Awareness is another word for boundlessness, for unicity, for seamlessness, for the unconditional love in which there is no separation between lover and beloved. In the light of awareness, whatever appears is the Holy Reality, for true love sees the perfection in everything just as it is.

No matter how bad our experience seems to get, even if the whole universe explodes, we know in our heart that nothing of substance has really been harmed. That which remains is unborn and indestructible. It is unnamable, but we could call it intelligence, energy, the Self, or simply *that* which has no opposite and no other. This boundless unicity or emptiness is uncaused. Nothing brings it about. It is always fully present. It is the whole dance of existence and it is what remains when everything perceivable and conceivable is no more.

When you dissolve into this groundless ground, there is only love—love for yourself, love for the world, love for all beings.

All there is arises all-at-once Here / Now in perfect stillness. The stars that are light-years away, the past, the future, all the different points of view, all the different movies that are playing—*everything* is Here / Now. *This* is the timeless eternity, the placeless presence, the all-inclusive unicity whose center is everywhere and whose circumference is nowhere. Here / Now is the groundless ground, the Ultimate Subject, the Original Face, that which remains in deep sleep when every experience disappears along with the mirage-like experiencer. No subject or object, no presence or absence remains.

And this Original Face is not something *other* than a bowl of soup or a cigarette butt in the gutter.

Is That All There Is?

*Someone once asked a Zen teacher, "What is
Buddha?"*

The teacher replied, "What is not Buddha?"

—unknown origin

Reality is not as it seems. Nor is it different.

—Lankavatara Sutra

When I point to the Holy Reality by drawing attention to
the sound of traffic, the song of a bird, the smell of coffee,
a cigarette butt in the gutter, or the hum of a vacuum
cleaner, people sometimes ask, Is that it? Is that all there
is? Traffic, birds, coffee, cigarette butts? Aren't we supposed to transcend all of that? Isn't that all an illusion or
just "the material world"? What about "Ultimate Reality"
and "supreme enlightenment"? Isn't the deepest truth
"prior to consciousness"? What about "the noumenon,"
"the soul," "God," "emptiness" or "pure awareness"?

Ultimate Reality is not somewhere else. Supreme
enlightenment is not somewhere else. The absolute is not
somewhere else. The Holy Reality is the intimacy, the
subtlety, the aliveness of Here / Now. *This* is God, *this* is
emptiness — *this* blue sky, *this* white cloud, *this* piece of
trash in the gutter, *this* armchair, *this* television program,

this leaf fluttering in the wind, *this* surge of anger, *this* yellow school bus, *this* wave of loneliness, *this* burst of laughter, *this* train of thought, *this* seeing-hearing-sensing-awaring-being. *This* is the Beloved.

A barking dog. Green leaves dancing in the sunlight. The listening silence. Open. Vast. Limitless. Just this!

This is not *like* anything else. It *is* as it is. How is it? It's not any particular way for it is always changing.

Writing about Ultimate Reality is like writing a book in disappearing ink.

If the words are really heard, they may open a door in the heart. They may bring our attention to the aliveness Here / Now. They may erase all our concepts and ideas and leave us open and full of wonder. But if the thinking mind gets stuck on trying to make sense of all this intellectually or *grasp* it conceptually, then the words only seem to take us farther away from the aliveness and the openness of presence.

The real message is what remains after the ink has vanished. But if you are looking to see what that is, you will never find it, for you are looking for an object. Presence is not an object. It is the openness that beholds it all.

What Is Looking Out of My Eyes?

The mirror reflects the image, but the image does not improve the mirror. You are neither the mirror nor the image in the mirror. Having perfected the mirror so that it reflects correctly, truly, you can turn the mirror round and see in it a true reflection of yourself—true as far as the mirror can reflect. But the reflection is not yourself—you are the seer of the reflection. Do understand it clearly—whatever you may perceive you are not what you perceive.

—Nisargadatta Maharaj

What we see when we look at one another and at anything we can see at all, including our own feet, is just our object. And our object is part of ourself as its subject. Nobody else can see us, because we have no objective existence whatsoever, and we cannot see anybody else because they have none.

—Wei Wu Wei

You *know* you are here. You know this beyond any shadow of a doubt. You need no authority to tell you this. You don't need to look in the mirror first. You don't need to go to school to learn this. You *know* you are here. You can't doubt your own being. By "you," I don't mean the character in the story of your life or what you've learned to *think* of as "you" or "your body" or "your mind," because all of that can be doubted. I simply mean this undeniable aware presence, this knowingness of being present, this present moment experiencing. *Hearing, seeing, sensing—being Here/Now. This* you cannot doubt. It is beyond doubt that you (as this aware presence) are here and that *something* is appearing here. We can argue about *what* this is (whether it is a dream or material reality, mind or matter, truth or illusion, this or that), but *that* it is, is undeniable. You can't doubt the *actuality* (or *suchness*) of this present event.

Awareness is the common factor in every experience. It is the experienc*ing* in every experience, the *seeing* that is equally present in (and *as*) everything that is seen, the hearing that is equally present in (and *as*) every sound. It is the *here-ness* of here, the *now-ness* of now, the undeniable *suchness* or *beingness* of this moment. We seemingly overlook it by looking *for* it, but we cannot actually overlook it or step outside of it. This beingness is all there really is, and wherever you look, you are always seeing yourself, the One Reality, ever-present and ever-changing.

This utterly immediate beingness is equally present in (and *as*) every experience: contracted experiences, expanded experiences, happy experiences, sad experiences, sunny days, thunderstorms, when there is thinking going on, when there is no thinking going on. This presence is the water in every wave, the mirror in every reflection, the seeing that can never be seen, the awareness beholding itself everywhere.

The so-called journey of spiritual awakening is not about arriving somewhere else or acquiring anything new. It is about recognizing what is most obvious, and *seeing through* (or waking up from) the false ideas and mirage-like imaginations that *seemingly* obscure what is right in front of us, most intimate, closer than our breath, impossible to *actually* avoid or overlook.

When we hear words like awakening or enlightenment, we tend to imagine that "I" might one day cross some magic line in the sand and become an "awakened person," forever after established in some perfect (and hopefully permanently pleasant) state. This is fantasy and illusion. This way of thinking is precisely what awakening wakes up from.

In fact, awakening or enlightenment is always only about Here / Now. *This* is the jewel beyond all price. This jewel is inconceivable and unimaginable not because it is something mysterious and esoteric and far away, but because it is so close, so all-inclusive, and so seemingly ordinary. Although this aware presence is invisible, it is visible everywhere! It is the whole universe, and it is what remains when the whole universe disappears.

Is the mind trying to grasp what that is? Is there a thought that "I don't get it"?

To awaken is to *see through* this movement of the thinking mind, and to simply *be* awake here and now, hearing the traffic sounds and the bird songs, breathing, seeing the colors and shapes of this moment. This is effortless because we can't *not* be here, present and aware, doing whatever we are doing. But thought has the ability to convince us that we are separate from our experience, that we are a fragment lost in an alien world, a ship on the ocean in danger of sinking. One very common way of *seemingly* overlooking the jewel is by *searching* for it "out there" somewhere.

Thus they say in Buddhism that if you see the Buddha on the road, kill it. In other words, if you imagine that Ultimate Reality is something outside of you, something you can objectify, something you can find or lose—a person, an event, an experience, a state, a memory, an idea, an understanding, a belief—then you must kill it. You must wake up. When you wake up, there is nothing outside of you. You are no-thing and everything.

If you try to pay attention *to* awareness or *to* the One Immutable Self, you objectify it—you make it into something outside of you. Whatever you imagine you see or find or experience is some subtle conceptual object. This same thing happens if you try to *identify* "yourself" with awareness. You objectify both "yourself" and "awareness," divide them (mentally) into two, and then try to merge these two (imaginary) objects and make them identical. This takes lots of mental efforting and imagination. And whatever experience of unity and expansion you manage to have, it inevitably disappears, leaving you with the belief that you've lost it and then the frustrating task of trying to recapture it.

On the other hand, if you stop all such convoluted efforts and simply relax into what is effortlessly occurring—hearing, seeing, sensing, breathing, awaring, being—then you realize you already *are* present as this whole undivided happening Here/Now. So instead of trying to *get* this, or *do* this, or *identify* as this, simply *be* this, which actually you can't *not* be. Even if a train of thought captures your attention and a mental movie unfolds in the imagination, this too is simply another movement of this undivided happening. Without awareness, it could not appear at all. But whenever the attention is completely absorbed, entranced and mesmerized by the *plotline* and the *content* of the mental movie story, then it *seems* as if there is a separate subject looking out at an objective world outside of itself—a ship on the sea in danger of sinking. Whenever attention goes instead to the bare perceiving of present moment sounds, sights, tastes, smells and somatic sensations, then there is simply one undivided happening. It's not that this kind of bare perception is "better" than being lost in thought, but you may discover that "you" (as a separate somebody) only exist *in* the mental movie story, not in the bare perceiving. In bare perceiving, there is one seamless happening with no center. There is diversity and variation in bare perceiving, but not separation.

The more deeply you go into any perception or sensation, the more clearly and vividly you experience non-solidity, impermanence, spaciousness, and emptiness. This direct experiencing reveals that everything is empty of substance and solidity. This ever-changing, ever-present experiencing is not *nothing* in a nihilistic sense. It is the no-*thing*-ness of this magnificently diverse, ever-changing seamlessness that can neither be grasped nor avoided.

So when there is confusion and seeking, when the mind is racing around on its imaginary treadmill desperately looking for the correct answers and straining to "get it," perhaps there will be a waking up from this habitual entrancement and a return to the utter simplicity of traffic sounds, the smell of rain, the hum of the refrigerator, the cool breeze on the skin, the blue sky reflected in a puddle on the sidewalk.

I'm not pointing to something mysterious or hard to get. I'm pointing to what is absolutely simple and obvious and unavoidable—the experiencing of this moment.

Only in thinking *about* this does the *apparent* separation and complication *seem* to arise.

No Self

*Events happen, deeds are done, but there is no
individual doer thereof.*

—The Buddha

What is reality? An icicle forming in fire.

—Dogen

*We're like whirlpools and music, hurricanes and
icicles. Once formed—that is, conceived—we're
seemingly particular things, yet in each moment, all
is fresh and new.*

—Steve Hagen

"No self" is not some exotic, mystical experience that
"you" have never had.

As we grow up, the undeniable *sense* of being present
and aware gets conflated with the *idea* of being a separate,
individual person located inside a particular bodymind.
What we actually *experience* every moment—boundless
being—gets *conceptually* divided up into subject and
object, self and other. The mirage-like separate "me," an
imaginary object, gets mistaken for the Ultimate Subject
(the unlocatable aware presence being and beholding it
all). Because we each seem to have our own unique movie

of waking life, we conclude that we are each a separate, independent unit of consciousness (a mind) encapsulated inside a separate body, looking out at an objective material world that is "out there," a world that each of us sees differently.

But is there a world "out there"? And is there a separate unit of consciousness (a mind) "in here"? If you are appearing in my movie, and I am appearing in your movie, could these apparently separate movies be like the jewels in Indra's Net, in which each is a reflection of all the others, or like a hologram where every part contains the whole?

There is a *thought*—an *idea*—that "I" am this person that I see in the mirror, this person with a name and a date of birth. There are pictures of "me" as a baby and a story of "me" being born and growing up. But all of these images and stories about "me" appear in awareness together with everything that is supposedly "not me"—the furniture, the rug, the computer, the other people, the clouds in the sky. It all shows up together as one whole seamless picture, a moving picture that is nothing but continuous change.

If we look closely, we discover that thinking happens by itself. Waking up from thoughts and fantasies happens by itself. Paying attention happens by itself. Making decisions happens by itself. Even what appears to be deliberate, premeditated, intentional action happens by itself. Thoughts arise, impulses arise, interests arise, action arises. *Everything* is one whole movement—the clouds, the street traffic, the thoughts, the blood flow, the galaxies deep in outer space, the infinite subatomic universes on the head of a pin—all of it is one undivided choiceless happening.

There is no actor apart from the action, no doer apart from the deed, no thinker apart from the thought, no "awarer" apart from awareness.

There is a functional identification with a particular form, a thought-sense of identity and location that coalesces and appears intermittently as needed (and sometimes dysfunctionally, when not really needed). In the movie of waking life, you know that you are playing Jane Doe and not Tom Brown. As Jane Doe, you appear to be located here on the couch and not over there on the other side of the room where Tom Brown is sitting. As Jane Doe, you appear to think things through, make choices and perform actions. That appearance is part of the functioning of life. You know whose name to answer to, which mouth to put the food in, how to cut the carrot and not your finger. If you had no functional sense of identity as Jane Doe, none of this would be possible. But this *functional* sense of identity, which appears intermittently as needed, is not the problem.

The problem—the source of our human suffering—is overlooking the bigger picture, the context in which this functional identification is occurring. We suffer because we imagine that we really *are* Jane Doe and *nothing but* Jane Doe, that what "I" truly am is a discrete unit of consciousness located inside a perishable and vulnerable body, located on one side of the room and not the other, struggling to survive as this separate fragment. We overlook our true identity as the awake space that is beholding and being *both* Jane Doe *and* Tom Brown *and* the entire universe, the seamlessness from which nothing stands apart, the unborn and indestructible boundlessness that is our True Nature. We believe instead that we are a finite "somebody," encapsulated and separate.

Believing ourselves to be an encapsulated fragment and imagining that we are in control of our lives leads to guilt and blame, worry over what "I" should do, feelings of failure and unworthiness, and the psychological fear of death (different from the instinctual fear that is a survival mechanism in a moment of danger).

But if you look more closely, you may discover that this present happening is not actually encapsulated or located anywhere in particular. You may find that any apparent boundary between one form and another, or between one location and another, turns out to be porous, mutable and ultimately simply not there. You may find that everything contains everything else, like a hologram, or like the jewels in Indra's Net.

Our usual understanding of impermanence is that the world is full of things, like tables and chairs and you and me, and that these things are all impermanent. But in Buddhism they say that the true understanding of impermanence reveals that there is actually no impermanence because nothing ever *forms* in the first place as a persisting, separate, independent "thing" to *be* impermanent. There is *only* thorough-going flux, seamless unicity—this ever-present, ever-changing Here/Now. This is what Buddhists mean by emptiness and what Advaita calls the one, immutable Self. When this is seen clearly, there is no fear of death, for there is no one separate to die. And there is no "me" to be unworthy or to fail.

But that doesn't mean that all sense of being a particular person will completely and permanently disappear. Like a mirage, this imaginary self will still appear under the right conditions, but once you know it's only a mirage, you don't have to take it quite as seriously when it shows up.

This mirage-like appearance of being a separate person *is*, in fact, absent much of the time in ordinary, everyday life. For example, as one is absorbed in reading a good novel, or driving down the freeway, or washing the dishes, whenever there is no thought-story about "me" playing in the mind, there is simply the happening of the moment: pages turning and the plot-story of the novel unfolding in the imagination, or cars and landscapes rushing past on the freeway, or soapy water sliding over dishes—sounds, sensations, movements of the bodymind all happening effortlessly. The "me" shows up only with the arising of a thought that posits a subject, for example, "*I* need to wash these dishes more quickly," or "*I* don't think *I* really understand the meaning of this novel."

Prior to those thoughts, there was no "me" in the picture, but this *me-less* experience in between thoughts is so ordinary that it is easily overlooked. Thought comes in very quickly and insists that, "*I* am reading the book," and this idea is supported by a visual image that the brain has learned to identify as "my hands holding the book," and there is a mental image of "me sitting in my armchair reading the book" that appears in the mind, and there is a whole thought-story that has been learned about "me and my eyes and my brain reading the book," and all of this together coalesces instantaneously into the *idea* that "*I* am reading the book," and this conceptual mirage *seems* like reality itself. Even to write about this, "I" am forced to use nouns and pronouns, thus further reinforcing the very illusion of solidity and separation that these words are attempting to expose. It takes a careful observation to see how this mirage of a separate self is created and re-created by language and thinking.

However absent or transparent the me-story becomes, a certain degree of functional identification with a particular bodymind will show up as needed in the play of life. What *may* completely and permanently disappear is that false sense of being "somebody" who is encapsulated and separate, the ship at sea in danger of sinking, the "me" who supposedly has to figure out "what I should do." Whether this mirage-like sense of being a separate self disappears intermittently or permanently doesn't really matter, except from the perspective of the imaginary "me" who wants to be a perfectly enlightened "me", completely "free of me." What a joke! From the perspective of the whole, it makes no difference. The whole includes everything. All of it is one, undivided, ownerless happening.

Even when a thought-story about "me" *appears* to create separation, encapsulation and ownership, this mirage-like appearance doesn't really have any solidity or substance. And *whatever* appears is gone in an instant. Our apparent problems can only persist *conceptually*, as ideas or stories. In reality, they are as ephemeral as snow-flakes. How serious can it all be?

But still, we *seem* to be separate, independent entities. After all, the mind reasons, I can't open your hand or feel your headache, so doesn't that prove that we are separate? Well, not really. I am no more conscious of the actions of "my" blood cells than I am of "your" headache, and I'm no more in control of "my" spleen than I am of the opening and closing of "your" hand. The boundary lines and the sense of ownership are conceptual abstrac-tions we learn.

Although there is no separate, independent self that is in control of "my life," that doesn't mean that there is no longer any discernable difference between an action that is entirely "out of my control" (such as the weather) and one that is apparently "in my control" (such as opening and closing my hand), or between an action that is voluntary and conscious (such as waving my arm) and one that is involuntary and unconscious (such as the functioning of my liver), or between an action that is reflexive and automatic (such as withdrawing my hand from a hot stove) and one that is the result of lengthy rumination and analysis (such as a carefully considered decision about accepting a job offer). These differences are discernable to anyone.

What falls away are the false *conclusions* we draw from these differences. Even the most apparently conscious, voluntary, intentional, well-reasoned, apparently freely-chosen and self-initiated action, when we begin to look closely at everything that was involved in making it happen, turns out to be the result of infinite causes and conditions that include everything from a leaf falling thirty years ago in New Jersey to the Big Bang. When we give any action careful attention as it unfolds, we can find no discernable "me" initiating it or carrying it out at any stage along the way. No one "chooses" to be a serial killer or to have a narcissistic personality disorder. Buddha had no choice about being Buddha, just as Hitler had no choice about being Hitler. The drug addict who recovers has no choice about recovering, just as the addict who doesn't recover has no choice about not recovering. Nothing could be other than it is in this moment. It is one undivided happening that includes Buddha *and* Hitler, recovering *and* not recovering, all as one inseparable event, one seamless ocean.

No wave is any wetter or any closer to the ocean than any other. In fact, no "wave" really even exists as a separate or persisting thing. There is simply waving. Maybe we could say that the universe is people-ing, as a kind of activity, but there are never any separate, discrete *people* in the way we think.

Is the Body Real? Am I the Body?

Let the body act as may suit it. Why are you so
concerned with it? Why do you pay attention to it?

—Ramana Maharshi

There is only a stream of sensations, perceptions,
memories and ideations. The body is an abstraction,
created by our tendency to seek unity in diversity....
It is like seeing the surface of the ocean and
completely forgetting the immensity beneath.

—Nisargadatta Maharaj

There is no contradiction between body and spirit,
between mind and matter. These are just words we
use to understand one thing.

—Zoketsu Norman Fischer

A wave does not have to stop being a wave in order
to be water.

—Thich Nhat Hanh

People steeped in spiritual ideas often say to me, "I know
I'm not the body." And I say, you *are* the body! That's not
all you are. You're not *limited* to the body or encapsulated
inside the body. You're *everything*! And no-*thing*. What

exactly *is* "the body" anyway? Look closely, and you'll find that "the body" is only a mental image, a concept, an abstraction.

Everything is changing, so what we call "a body" (or "a river" or "a chair" or "a mountain") is not really the same "thing" from one instant to the next. No continuous form exists or stands apart from everything else in the universe. Everything is one undivided, boundless event.

Tune into sensing rather than thinking, and it is immediately clear that this so-called "body" is not a solid, enduring *thing* at all. It's a mass of ever-changing, vibrating, pulsing sensations and activities. In the world of sensation, you cannot actually find where this body begins and ends. No boundary between "your body" and "the room in which you are sitting" can be located in sensation. The boundary is conceptual.

Close your eyes and explore the "boundary" between your body and the chair. You can find sensations, but where in those sensations do "you" end and where does "the chair" begin?

As you breathe, look to see where the border is between "inside of you" and "outside of you." Do you find an actual place, a solid border, a real boundary of any kind?

When we *think* about the body, it seems solid and persisting and separate from everything else. When we *sense* the body instead, we discover ever-changing, undivided formlessness or flux.

The difference between thinking and sensing is like the difference between an anatomy book and a living person. Cut open a living person and everything is moving and pulsating and slippery and changing shape. It's not neat and tidy and fixed and clearly delineated like the anatomy book, and it doesn't hold still because it's alive! The world created by thought is like the anatomy book. It's abstract and frozen. Sensation is alive, ephemeral, vibrating, moving, ever-changing, ungraspable. But even thinking, the raw *actuality* of it as it is happening, is equally alive, ephemeral, moving, ever-changing, and ungraspable—every thought is an energetic flash that is gone almost before it arrives. But the *content* that thinking unfolds in the imagination, the picture-story that thought paints, *that* is what *seems* solid and fixed, although if you look closely, you see that even that is nothing but flux. Your stories, beliefs, opinions, ideas and self-images are always changing.

In fact, your body includes the entire universe because nothing is really separate from anything else. Your body is dependent upon and made up of sunlight, water, air, food, stardust and atomic energy—we could say that the whole universe is appearing as you. And furthermore, you might notice that the whole universe is appearing *in* you, isn't it? When you look for the boundary between "you" (aware presence) and "the world out there" (perceptions and sensations), between "perceiver" and "perceived," between "inside" and "outside," between "subject" and "object," what do you find? This imaginary boundary that we call "I" is an idea, a mental image, a kind of mirage, isn't it?

The "I am not the body" pointer that we hear in many spiritual teachings is an attempt to point beyond the illusion of encapsulation and separation. It is an attempt to question the exclusive identification with the body as what "I" am and the tendency to take the body (its condition, appearance, tendencies, behaviors and abilities) personally. The "I am not the body" pointer is an attempt to point out that "the body" is a concept we have learned, *not* our actual present moment *experience,* which is actually boundless and seamless, ever-changing flux.

But instead, the "I am not the body" pointer often seems to inadvertently point people toward dissociation and some disembodied notion of being nobody or nothing. People get the idea that they aren't supposed to care about the body (or the world), that the body is merely some kind of illusion to be discarded or ignored. The real illusion is how we *think* about the body, how we conceptualize and abstract it, how we imagine it to be solid, separate, independent and persisting. And above all, how we imagine an owner who occupies the body, a "me" who is encapsulated inside, steering the body through life like a car or a ship. This "me" wants to get enlightened and is therefore supposed to "not identify as the body," and is instead trying to identify itself as pure awareness. That "me" that thinks it has to identify or not identify as this or that is the root illusion. But the body itself is totally real. Not the conceptualized body that we think about and imagine. But the *actual* body, which is no-thing that can be grasped or separated out from everything else. The real body is pure experiencing, pure being, pure awareness. It is the whole universe.

I have found working *with* the body to be one of the most powerful ways of realizing boundlessness. Martial arts training and other movement practices, singing, chanting, dancing, lovemaking, meditative explorations of bodily sensation, somatic awareness work such as Feldenkrais—these have all been profoundly liberating, transformative and enjoyable. Working or playing with the body can dissolve imaginary limitations and reveal the wholeness of being in ways that cannot be grasped or formulated by thought. These nonconceptual explorations happen on a deeper level than the cognitive mind.

Our suffering is mental and conceptual—it is all about the stories in our heads—the map-world rather than the territory itself. Anything that brings us out of our heads, out of our mental spinning, and into the aliveness of non-conceptual presence and awareness is potentially very liberating.

Go deeply into the body and you'll find no body at all. In every sense.

Not Taking Your Life Personally: What Does That Mean?

The universe is full of action, but there is no actor.

—Nisargadatta Maharaj

When nondual teachings speak of not taking the events of our life personally (not "taking delivery," as Nisargadatta used to say), or when these teachings say that "the person" is a kind of mirage, this isn't meant to *deny* the apparent person in every sense or to suggest that "enlightened people" turn into amorphous blobs of indistinguishable nothingness without feelings or personalities. It doesn't mean you have to drop your name and go around insisting you are nobody, nor does it mean that if your wife dies, the goal is to be untouched and not "take it personally."

What is being pointed to is not detachment or insensitivity, but rather, total intimacy, unfiltered sensitivity—the absence of separation—nonduality. Nothing exists independently of everything else, and everything is nothing but ceaseless change. When we are born, this seamless immediacy is obvious, although of course we don't conceptualize or formulate it in words at that stage of life. But when we are first born, there is simply open aware presence and the undivided happening of the moment—hunger flows into food flows into sleep flows into sounds and shapes and colors and warmth and movement. As far as we are concerned at that stage of life, we have no name, no age, no gender, no race, no nationality, no social class, no purpose, no flaws, no story. We *learn* all of those things, and we learn to *think* of ourselves as a separate, persisting individual encapsulated inside a bodymind, somebody *apart* from this world who was born *into* this world, somebody who "looks out" at the world and who lives "in" it. But this separation is conceptual. When we look for this "body" or this "mind" or this "person" or "this world," all we actually find is thorough-going flux and ceaseless change, in which everything is inseparable from everything else.

That undivided, boundless experiencing that the baby has, in which life is perceived as one whole undivided happening, is still here, but in the adult, that experience of unbroken wholeness has been overlaid and to some degree obscured by all the concepts that have been learned and then super-imposed on top of the bare simplicity of present experiencing. We have learned to focus on the map instead of the territory. We *overlook* what is most intimate, most obvious, most undeniable—our actual present moment *experiencing*, as it is—and we focus instead on the stories, labels, ideas, beliefs, explanations and abstract categories *about* it—the conceptual map.

Let's take an example. "Chicago" is a word, a concept, a label, an object on a map. But to what actual *territory* does this word refer? We cannot deny that there is *something* we call Chicago, but when we start to look closely at what exactly this something is, we find that we can't pin down exactly what "Chicago" is, for it is always in flux, and it's borders are, in reality, nonexistent, changing and completely permeable. The sign "Welcome to Chicago" proclaims a legal boundary, but on the ground itself (or in the air), you don't actually find any separation between Chicago and the city next to it. The earth itself is a continuous, undivided process, as is the air. The lake that borders Chicago on one side moves in and out with the tides and the waves, making it utterly impossible to pin down an *actual* place where Chicago ends and Lake Michigan begins. Only on the map does Chicago look like a solid, clearly delineated object. But in reality, it is nothing but unbounded, ceaseless change. We can't *deny* Chicago, but we can't really get hold of it either.

We can't deny that Chicago has a unique and distinct personality, a flavor entirely different from San Francisco, London, Bombay or any other city. But again, we can't pin down exactly *what* that personality is, for it, too, is always changing and showing different faces of itself. Different people see it differently. If you're in Chicago, or more accurately, if Chicago shows up Here / Now, this happening called Chicago has an undeniable reality—smells, sounds, textures, colors, shapes, movements—but all of this is a fleeting appearance that cannot be grasped or held onto. It has no inherent, substantial, persisting, objective reality. Even the buildings that seem so solid are slowly decomposing.

And what about the weather? We don't take the weather in Chicago personally—we don't *blame* the city for having a cloudy day. We don't feel the city clouded up deliberately through an act of independent free will, that it was "out to get us," or that it "wasn't trying hard enough" to be sunny. Instead, we recognize that a cloudy day is the result of innumerable causes and conditions that have no owner, no author, no actor.

Likewise, we cannot deny that there is someone we call Joan who has a unique personality. But we can't get hold of exactly *what* this "Joan" is, or where exactly she begins and ends, or what exactly her personality *is*, for all of this is changing and moving and inseparable from everything else in the universe that is supposedly "not Joan." If we really see the seamlessness and interbeing of everything, and the way it is all an ever-changing appearance, then we realize that there is no independent executive at the helm inside Joan who *chooses* her cloudy weather anymore than there is any such entity inside the city of Chicago. We don't blame Joan for being the way she is, nor do we waste time trying to turn her into somebody else, just as we wouldn't try to turn Chicago into Los Angeles. We recognize that the unique weather patterns we call "Joan" are the result of innumerable causes and conditions.

It is in that sense that we speak of not taking our weather personally and that we talk about the separate person being nothing but a mirage. But we don't *deny* that there is something here that we call Joan or that she has a distinct personality. We also would not deny that this organism called Joan can apparently open and close her hand whenever she wants to—but when we look closely for the source of the impulse and ability to perform that action, we find no central executive at the helm. The whole universe is showing up as this opening and closing of the hand and this unfolding event called Joan.

So when you hear that the person is a kind of mirage, or that the body is a conceptual idea, or that you don't need to take your life personally, these kinds of statements point to the fluidity, the wholeness, the emptiness that is Here / Now. It doesn't mean that you don't grieve if your spouse dies or that you no longer have so-called "boundaries" in a psychological or social sense. It doesn't mean you lose all your personality traits or all your neurotic quirks. It doesn't mean you don't apologize when you hurt someone or make a mistake, or that you don't still have opinions and preferences, or that you don't ever set goals or make an effort or care about anything. It doesn't mean that you can't open and close your hand or shift your focus of attention seemingly "at will," or that you lose all functional sense of identity as a particular bodymind, or that you can't tell the difference between yourself and your computer. *It just means that you don't take any of this personally.* In fact, you may actually *feel* life much more deeply when you don't take it personally. This isn't about being "impersonal" in the sense of being detached, dissociated or uninvolved. It isn't about *withdrawing* from life or *denying* your humanness. Quite the opposite. It is total intimacy—*no separation*. You recognize that *all* of this (your grief, your neurosis, your opinions, your actions) is one whole seamless happening, inseparable from the wind, the trees, the oceans, the tides, the planets, the stars, the galaxies, the black holes and the awareness that beholds it all.

What Is This?

In any so-called moment, there is only a totally unformed, inexplicable happening.

—Darryl Bailey

Descriptions are many and contradictory. Reality is simple.... It is only when you try to describe and explain, that the words fail you.

—Nisargadatta Maharaj

Take a moment once again to stop reading and to simply appreciate the happening of this moment. Be fully present to the sounds, fragrances, aromas, visual images, somatic sensations—not these labels, but the happening itself, this undeniable and utterly immediate present experiencing. *What is this?*

The thinking mind instantly wants to supply an answer. It wants to figure this out—label everything, categorize it, explain it, understand it, analyze it, capture it, frame it, get control of it. This is the function of the thinking mind, and it serves us well in certain basic survival situations such as food-gathering, shelter-building, or navigating our way through new terrain. It has gotten us to the moon and to the top of the food chain. Our conceptual maps are functionally necessary and not to be discarded, but no matter how accurate the map is, it is never the territory itself. And yet, we have a deeply-conditioned tendency to mistake the map for the territory. We do this without even realizing we are doing it.

Some of our most commonplace concepts are so ubiquitous and pervasive that we lose sight of the fact that they are actually concepts. "The world," "the body," "the mind," "the self," "consciousness," "awareness," "nonduality"—we throw these word-concepts around without ever stopping to wonder what we are actually talking about. And next thing we know, we're lost in some conceptual confusion, very much akin to wondering what will happen to me if I step off the edge of the flat earth. That's an imaginary problem, as all of us in the 21st century realize, but for people in earlier centuries, it seemed quite real. And our own conceptual conundrums seem equally real to us. "Will I still be here after I die?" or "Am I enlightened yet?" or "Do I have free will?" can seem like perfectly sensible questions, but they are every bit as absurd as wondering what will happen to me when I step off the edge of the earth.

Thought divides the world up into pieces and then tries to figure out which comes first, the chicken or the egg (the brain or consciousness, mind or matter), as if this problem actually makes sense, as if the "things" we are trying to reconcile actually exist. Conceptual thought serves us well as long as we don't forget that the conceptual pictures it generates are at best only *relatively* true, but never *absolutely* true. For example, "The earth is a planet orbiting the sun." This is a relative truth. It is functionally useful. We're certainly not going to *deny* it. But in the absolute sense, there is no such *thing* as an "earth" or a "sun," for these are conceptual abstractions of what is actually ever-changing, inconceivable, undivided, unknowable, seamless flux, a fleeting appearance in consciousness.

When we try to figure out "the meaning of life" or "the nature of reality," or when we try to come up with a conceptual understanding of Consciousness, Totality, God, or the Ground of Being, we inevitably end up frustrated and confused. Any conceptual picture of reality is always subject to doubt, and no metaphysical formulation ever satisfies our deep longing for Truth.

What satisfies that deep longing of the heart is the falling away of the attempt to make sense of everything. Of course, that doesn't mean we don't still make relative sense of things in a functional way in daily life. But we stop trying to take hold of Totality, or grasp the Ground of Being, or figure out the meaning of life. Instead, we relax into simply *being* life. We learn to recognize (to *see*, to *sense*) when we're beginning to grasp or fixate, and in that recognition, quite naturally there is an ability to relax and let go. When we stop trying to figure it all out, we discover that it doesn't *need* to be figured out, and in fact, *can't* be figured out! When we stop desperately trying to get a grip, we find nothing is lacking and there is nothing to grasp.

When we wake up to simply *being* Here / Now, all our confusion and problems vanish into thin air. Of course, we may still have a flat tire or a terminal cancer, but it is no longer a problem. There is nothing confusing about it. Our neurotic habits, our so-called character defects, our apparent imperfections, mistakes and failings— all of this is realized to be simply the weather of life, and it is no more personal or meaningful than a cloudy day.

It is a passing appearance, and in the next moment, it all changes.

Thought and language are wonderful tools. But words are inherently abstract and representational. Even when they are trying not to, they inevitably tend to freeze and divide the seamless fluidity of life, creating the mirage-like conceptual appearance of separate, independent forms that persist through time. So whenever we try to *think* about life, we tend to get easily confused. We get confused because we are thinking about and trying to reconcile "things" that don't actually exist. Whatever verbal formulation we use to describe reality is never quite right. Thought can never get hold of the *actuality* of *this-here-now*. Reality itself is too fluid, too immediate, too dynamic to be divided up and caught in the conceptual net of words.

If we say, "This is it," the words *create* the very split they attempt to point beyond. If we say "All is One," it is one too many. If we call it "nothing," it seems to deny the undeniable presence of *everything*. If we assert that "there is nothing to do," it seems to overlook the necessity of doing whatever we are moved by life to do. If we assert that "there *is* something to do," it makes it sound as if something else is required in order to be what we already are.

The dualistic mind grasps, reifies, asserts, denies and fixates. It takes positions and clings to those positions, mistaking them for reality. It *identifies* with its positions and feels threatened when they are questioned. But to cling to *any* conceptual map of reality is to miss the ever-changing actuality of *this-here-now*.

That doesn't mean we can't still use words. Words can be helpful pointers, but if we think that "Here / Now" or

"Awareness" or "emptiness" or "the Self" or "the Tao" or "Buddha Nature" or "Oneness" or "Unicity" is some relative "thing" that we can grasp, then we have made the absolute into just another illusory object. But what these words all point to is not *something*. It is the no-*thing*-ness (the emptiness, the seamlessness, the boundlessness, the unformed nature) of everything. Emptiness (or unicity) cannot be perceived as an object in the way that we can perceive a mirror, a movie screen or an ocean, which is why these analogies all fall short at a certain point. On the other hand, paradoxically, there is nothing we can see and nowhere we can look that is *not* emptiness.

When we stop trying to grasp or control our present experience in *any* way, when we are completely willing for it to be exactly as it is, then something shifts.

The illusory bubble pops. We see that Here / Now is always unobstructed, boundless and open. It is open enough to include even resistance and contraction. Contraction is simply another form that formlessness is momentarily assuming, another fleeting appearance with no inherent reality. Nothing needs to be different from how it is. We don't need to define or explain this present happening, and in fact, we can't!

The only real answer to "What is this?" is to be awake and see.

Not Making Something Out of Nothing & Not Making Nothing into Something

If nothing is permanent, what can be impermanent, both, or neither?

—Nagarjuna

Is it that there are various ways of seeing one object, or is it that we have mistaken various images for one object?

—Dogen

Experience takes place only in the present, and beyond and apart from experience nothing exists.

—Ramana Maharshi

There is a great difference in having the belief that you are not the author and not having the belief that you are the author.

—Wayne Liquorman

True emptiness is letting go of fixed ideas, seeing through (not discarding or renouncing, but *seeing through*) all our beliefs, waking up to the groundlessness of Here / Now. Emptiness could also be described as the spaciousness, the openness, the aliveness of non-conceptual presence.

We can be so easily hypnotized by our metaphors, words, concepts and analogies—even those concepts that are intended to wake us up from this hypnosis. Thought is always trying to get a grip, rather than relaxing into the concept-free emptiness of Here / Now.

The great Buddhist teacher Nagarjuna was noted for pointing out the fallacies in every possible way in which we try to conceptualize and take hold of reality. He did this without ever offering the *right* way of conceptualizing it. The mind desperately wants the right formulation, but Nagarjuna never provided that. He recognized that concepts can't ever be the truth. If we assert that there *is* a self or there *isn't* a self, or that there *is* free will or there *isn't* free will, it is never quite right because words simply cannot capture the fluidity and ungraspability of everything. To let go of all fixed positions and hold onto nothing, to abide in non-conceptual presence—*this* is emptiness.

Consciousness by its very nature is always making something out of nothing—that's what consciousness does (or *is*)—and the conceptualizing (grasping) mind even wants to take hold of "nothing" and make that, too, into an even bigger *something* that we can put on our altar and worship. But *anything* perceivable or conceivable is only another fleeting appearance in this undivided happening.

We try to grasp this ever-changing, nonconceptual actuality with concepts, or we chase after special experiences and states of mind, seeking transcendence where it can never be found. True nonduality is not about special experiences or correct formulations. It is *just this,* right here, right now.

To be awake is to abide in inconceivability and groundlessness. It is the absence of grasping and fixating. It is the willingness to live without handles and footholds, to remain in the question without seeking an answer. To be awake is to be open.

Hearing wind in leaves, there is no persisting form, no division, no separation, no "me" apart from the wind, no listener apart from the sound, no sound "out there" apart from the listening presence. Without thought, there is simply the immediacy of *whooooooosh!*

Thought comes in afterwards and says: "I hear wind in leaves." Instantly, a whole conceptual picture takes shape in the mind like a mirage, a picture in which we suddenly *seem* to have subjects and objects, causes and effects, and actors who exist independently of their actions. In this conceptual mirage, "I" am worrying about getting enlightened, and thought insists that there must be something more to Ultimate Reality than "just" that whooshing sound. *That* can't be enough! Thought begins chasing something bigger and better to fill the sense of lack and uncertainty that it has just created! It imagines "Ultimate Reality" as *something* it hopes to find, a final understanding, a special experience, something *other* than Here / Now. Round and round the thinking mind goes on its treadmill, chasing the imaginary carrot.

But the nondual absolute is that simple, immediate, nonconceptual *whoooosh*. And eventually we see that even thoughts and the mirage-worlds they spin are also a kind of energetic *whoosh,* and that *nothing* is outside that boundless totality. Even the mirage of solidity and separation is nothing but *whooshing*.

But only in thought do we *apparently* have a "seer" and something "out there" that is being seen. Our actual *experiencing* is simply undivided *seeing*, with no boundary between subject and object. This is not a philosophy to believe in, but a palpable reality to recognize. If we cling to the *philosophy* that there is "no subject and no object," that is just more baggage, another belief to defend or doubt.

Anyone can easily dispense the correct nondual answers once you catch on and get the hang of it. This can momentarily feel very satisfying: "Now I've got it all figured out. Everything is unicity." But if this word "unicity" is only another form of fixation and grasping, then in the next moment, the mind will begin to doubt: "Maybe it's not all unicity. How do we know it is?" The word is only a word. If we say, "Everything is Bloopity-Bloop," it is immediately obvious that we haven't really said anything at all! And the same thing is true when we say, "Everything is unicity."

At their best, words emerge out of emptiness and dissolve back into emptiness, like arrows that self-destruct on impact, dissolving the target. But words can also emerge from or inadvertently trigger the grasping mind and be a subtle (or not so subtle) movement away from the openness (and perceived vulnerability) of bare being, a movement into the (safer, in the mind's view) mental world of thought-structures and belief systems designed to provide comfort, zest, meaning, security and whatever else we feel is lacking Here / Now. When that happens, words solidify and construct illusions rather than dissolving and deconstructing them.

Of course, in the absolute sense, there is no division, constructing or deconstructing—it's all unicity, but again, it's easy to *say* that. But the menu never satisfies our hunger. The aliveness of presence, the spaciousness and immediacy of being, *this* alone satisfies our deepest longing, for this alone is real.

Waking up is about letting go of everything, not holding on to something. So be aware of how easy it is to make something out of nothing, and to make "Nothing" into something. If you sense yourself holding onto some great idea or comforting notion, or some particular experience or state of mind, let it go.

There's an old Zen dialog where the Zen master keeps telling his student to "drop it!" and finally the student says he has nothing left to drop, and the master says, "drop that!"

In another old Zen story, the teacher and student have been talking into the night, and finally the teacher tells the student it's time for the student to leave and go back to his sleeping quarters. The student opens the door and says, "It's very dark outside." The teacher offers the student a lighted candle to find his way home. Just as the student receives the light, the teacher blows it out.

Not One, Not Two

Before I took up Zen, there were mountains and valleys. After I began the practice of Zen, there were no mountains and no valleys. In enlightenment, there are mountains and valleys.

—Old Zen story

The Buddha way is, basically, leaping clear of the many and the one.

—Dogen

Beware of clinging to one half of a pair.

—Huang Po

Just as all waves are the undivided movement of one ocean, everything in the universe is a seamless and boundless unicity. Mountains and valleys are one flowing event that cannot be pulled apart. Sages have called this the One Self or the One Mind. This all-inclusive and undivided unicity is all there is, and all there is, is this. Seeing through the illusion of separation is an essential realization on the pathless path of liberation. At the same time, it is obvious to anyone that apples are not oranges and that mountains are not valleys. Thus, the truth is said to be not one, not two.

Our ordinary, dualistic perspective is that there is somebody ("me") who is "in here" looking out at a separate, independent, objective world that is "out there." This external world seems to be full of countless separate objects and millions of people, each of whom is presumed to be an independent entity with free will.

If we take up meditation, or if we read books on nonduality, or if we simply begin to look more closely, we discover that there is no actual boundary between "in here" and "out there," that everything is one inseparable whole, that there is no "me." We begin to notice what is the same in every different experience. We realize there are no mountains and no valleys, no self and no other-than-self.

But if we cling to oneness and deny multiplicity, if we become attached to emptiness, this is still dualistic, for we are sticking to one side of an imaginary divide. At the root of that attachment, there is still a sense of somebody who is holding on to being nobody. True enlightenment has no investment in being nobody. It sees wholeness but doesn't deny or overlook differences. The nondual absolute *includes* relative reality but is not bound or confused by it. Unicity *includes* the ability to distinguish mountains from valleys. It *includes* the experience of being a particular person in the play of life. Being awake is seeing *both* the relative truth in any life situation *and* the absolute truth and not getting fixated on or stuck in either one. True nondualism recognizes that mountains and valleys are one inseparable event *and* it can tell the difference between them. Nondualism doesn't deny either aspect of the whole truth.

In practical terms, what does this mean? It means that we don't have to try really hard not to be a person or to obliterate all our desires, opinions and preferences. It means that if we have certain responsibilities on our job, it probably isn't a great idea to tell our boss that there is no one to carry out these responsibilities and no choice about whether they get done or not. If a mother is grieving the death of her only child, telling her that her child was only a mirage and that nothing has actually died may not be the clearest expression of nonduality at that moment. If we yell hurtful things at our partner, when we recognize what we've done, it's natural to feel remorse and regret and to apologize. This is the action of life itself. In many ordinary situations such as these, to fixate exclusively on absolute truth and ignore relative reality can actually be a form of evasion, dishonesty, lack of compassion or downright stupidity. Context matters.

When we are awake as boundless presence, when we know that there is nothing and no one to defend, when we realize that we contain the whole universe, then acknowledging and apologizing for our mistakes is a much more natural and likely response than regurgitating nondual platitudes. Defensiveness, guilt and blame arise out of and feed the misconception that we are all separate, independent selves in control of our lives. But regret, sorrow, compassion and response-ability are the natural by-products of being awake and seeing clearly.

Mountains and valleys (enlightenment and delusion, relative and absolute, good and evil, self and not-self) are conceptual abstractions of what is actually seamless flux. They only exist relative to each other. They are a display in consciousness. Consciousness *is* the dividing up of the undivided, the forming of the formless, the making visible the invisible. All forms that appear are nothing but formless movement, one seamless whole from which nothing stands apart. And yet, relatively speaking, in the movie of waking life, we don't confuse a mountain with a valley.

Clarity and confusion are aspects of one inseparable whole *and* we can discern a difference between them. There is only the timeless, ever-present Now *and* there is history, evolution, and planning for the future. I am boundless awareness *and* I am Joan. Everything is perfect and complete as it is *and* I can change a flat tire or send my children to school to get an education. *Both* sides of the coin are true. Zen masters have called this realization "the merging of difference and unity" or "groundlessness." Enlightenment *sees* that mountains and valleys are "not one, not two." As my first Zen teacher put it, "You are perfect just as you are, but that doesn't mean there is no room for improvement."

What Should I Do?

*More than any other time in history, mankind faces
a crossroads. One path leads to despair and utter
hopelessness. The other, to total extinction. Let us
pray we have the wisdom to choose correctly.*

—Woody Allen

*I found that things became a lot easier when I
no longer expected to win. You abandon your
masterpiece and you sink into the real Masterpiece.*

—Leonard Cohen

*Everybody behaves according to his nature. It cannot
be helped, nor need it be regretted.*

—Nisargadatta

*All that anyone can ever do is be the body, need,
interest, urge, and action that nature is presenting in
any particular moment.*

—Darryl Bailey

*What you do, I am doing; what you have done,
I have done. No one is doing it—everything is
happening on its own in vast open space.*

—Toni Packer

When we take our life personally and identify exclusively as the bodymind character, and when we believe the popular notion that this character is endowed with free will, then it feels like a huge weight, trying to "do the right thing" and win the game, whether the game is making money, saving the world, or getting enlightened. We feel tremendous pressure to figure out, "What should I do?" *As if* there is someone here calling the shots and directing the show, *as if* we could screw it up and single-handedly ruin the universe, *as if* we have a choice, *as if* there is more than one possibility Here / Now, *as if* we are a ship in danger of sinking.

But *are* we actually authoring our thoughts, deciding what to think, what to want, what to do? Or is that whole picture of an executive self with free will nothing more than how we have learned to *conceptualize* and *think about* our experience? This map positing a self with free will is so widely accepted as reality that not many people ever question it. To many people, it seems like a very dangerous thing to question. But more and more, neuroscience is confirming the absence of an executive self. The ancient Zen masters and Advaita sages discovered this absence without the benefit of quantum physics or 21st century neuroscience. They relied on direct experience, which is what intelligent meditation or meditative inquiry is really all about.

When we look for the source of our breathing, or the source of our words as we are speaking, or the source of our thoughts as they pop up, or if we look to see what is aware of being aware, we may experience a kind of brief apperception of nothingness, a popping of the bubble of separation, a sense of boundlessness, as if everything graspable has suddenly vanished into thin air, a momentary sense of free-falling in empty space.

This experience in itself is not important. What matters is the discovery that we cannot actually locate the source of our thoughts, impulses and actions. When we look closely, we find that we cannot really say how we do the simplest things, such as opening and closing our hand or reading the words on this page, nor can we find anyone doing these actions as they happen. They simply *happen*.

Did you "choose" to have the political leanings you have, or the sexual preferences you have, or the interests and passions, the talents and abilities? Are you *choosing* which activities you are drawn to do, or which people you find attractive and interesting to be with, or which sources of news and information seem trustworthy to you and which do not? Did you "decide" to be interested in the questions that brought you to this book?

As someone who has had a long history of addiction and compulsion, I understand firsthand how powerful these forces are, and I also know that countless forces of nature and nurture go into producing them. It is easy to view them as moral or spiritual failings and to blame ourselves or others for not being able to "snap out of it" at will or "just say no." But in fact, we can't always "snap out of it." To simply tell people, as some spiritual teachings do, that we have a choice, that we create our own reality, that anyone can "choose" to be rich and successful or to stop an addiction, that if we are suffering it is because we are choosing to suffer, such assertions easily pour salt into the wound. These notions are especially cruel when someone has been trying for decades to become the person they think they should be, longing to be free of a particular compulsive pattern, trying every self-improvement method and treatment option under the sun, all to no avail.

Thought imagines a God "out there" and a self "in here" at the controls, calling the shots. In fact, if you look closely, you discover that no independent entity can be found either "out there" or "in here" who is running the show or freely choosing what to want, what to think, what to care about, and what to do. When your car gets a flat tire and you respond in whatever way you do at that moment, that response is the movement of life, as is the tire going flat. Action happens, apparent choices occur, but there is no actor behind the action, no chooser behind the choices, no decider behind the decisions, no thinker behind the thoughts, no seer behind the seeing. To realize this directly is to wake up from the trance of blame, shame, guilt, retribution and vengeance, all of which are predicated on the notion that there is an executive at the helm inside every bodymind, an independent unit of consciousness, a self that is freely choosing what to do.

When we understand this clearly, it doesn't mean we won't still put serial killers in prison or do everything possible to keep child molesters away from children, but perhaps we won't need to shame and blame these unfortunate people as well. Perhaps we can see the serial killer or the child molester with compassion, knowing that, "There, but for the grace of God, go I." And perhaps we will treat ourselves with compassion if we fail to measure up to our own ideals.

This understanding doesn't in any way advocate denial or not "taking responsibility" in the sense of recognizing and acknowledging our mistakes, doing what we can to apologize or put things right, and perhaps taking a different course of action going forward *(if we can)*. It points rather to the possibility of understanding that in every moment we are doing the only thing possible at that moment and so is everyone else. None of what happens is personal.

This doesn't mean not having opinions, but rather, having them in a bigger context. For example, if someone thinks that homosexuality or gender variance is an abomination against God, or that climate change is a hoax, or that white people should rule the world—I will most certainly disagree with that person. In some instances, I may try to change that person's mind or do whatever I can to see that he or she doesn't act out of these views in ways that are harmful, but there will also be a recognition that this person is no more "choosing" to have the views that he has than I am "choosing" to have an opposite set of views. This absence of choice doesn't mean this person might not change his mind in the next moment, but if he does, it won't be because of free will, for no such thing actually exists. Although this person's worldview is ignorant and wrong from my perspective; nonetheless, I can see that there is a place in this universe for everything that appears. After all, it's all here! From the perspective of evolution and the survival of the species, the checks and balances provided by people with different ideologies may serve some kind of survival function, or from the perspective of Cosmic Entertainment, it may just make for good drama. But in one way or another, it's all part of the dance. It's all happening. It is as it is. Seeing this bigger picture doesn't mean I won't still have my opinions or play my part, but there will also be a recognition that all of us are an expression of One Self, that together we make up one whole vision and one whole movement, that everything is an aspect of the same infinite Self-realization, all of it one dance, and that in every moment, each of us is doing the only thing possible at that moment.

Does this mean that the *next* moment is already determined? Can we see that the "next moment" is actually only a fantasy?

Choice and Choicelessness

Are you breathing? Or are you being breathed? You need not answer. There is no essential difference.

—Steve Hagen

I seemingly "made a choice" almost forty years ago to stop drinking alcohol excessively. I had been an addictive drinker and heavy drug user for the better part of a decade in my late teens and early twenties. Given the amount of different things I consumed and the high-risk behavior I engaged in, it is truly a miracle that I lived through this time in my life. I could easily have died or been killed on many occasions, and I could easily have killed someone else. I had frequent black-outs, was often violent, would wake up in jail or in the hospital or in bed with someone I had no memory of ever seeing before. And then suddenly one day, I knew it was over. By sheer coincidence, at a medical appointment for something else, I ran into a physician-therapist who specialized in working with alcoholics and drug addicts. I had heard of her, and right there on the spot, I asked her to help me sober up. She agreed. At that moment, I knew something had irrevocably shifted, that my days as a drunk were over.

My therapist approached addiction not as a disease over which I was powerless, but rather as a behavior that I was unconsciously choosing to do for a variety of reasons. She believed that I could become consciously aware of how I was making this choice and what I was getting out of drinking. I could then consciously make a different choice not to destroy myself, and I could learn new ways to do whatever positive things I was relying on alcohol to accomplish such as releasing creativity and relaxing inhibitions. My therapist thought that permanent abstinence was not always necessary and that a once-alcoholic-drinker could learn to drink in moderation after dealing with the underlying causative issues in therapy. We worked together for a year and my life changed dramatically. Initially, I stopped drinking completely. Then, with the permission of my therapist, I tried drinking in moderation. There were a few stumbles, but for the most part, it seemed to work perfectly.

For the next nearly three decades, I rarely drank or even thought about drinking, and I never again did recreational drugs. I had smoked several packs of cigarettes a day during the years I was drinking heavily, and I stopped smoking completely. I formed new friendships and moved into social circles where people either never drank or did so only in moderation and where no one ever did recreational drugs. I studied martial arts, practiced Zen, earned a graduate degree in creative writing, lived and worked at a meditation retreat center, wrote books and articles about awareness and nonduality. For almost three decades, I lived a life of sobriety. On rare occasions, I had a glass of wine with dinner, but years went by between one drink and the next. Alcohol was a non-issue.

Then after all these years of sobriety, somewhere in the hormonal upheaval of menopause and the emotional upheaval of my mother dying, there were several years where I engaged, off and on, in addictive drinking, a pattern I had been completely certain was gone for good. The drinking wasn't nearly as extreme or as destructive as what I'd done decades before. I wasn't drinking in bars at all hours of the day and night. I wasn't putting away massive amounts of hard liquor combined with drugs and cigarettes. I wasn't having fist fights or waking up in jail with no memories from the night before. This was a few glasses of wine on some evenings, not every evening, in the privacy of my own home. Sometimes, I could have just one glass of wine and stop there, but more often I had two and sometimes even three glasses. Occasionally, I finished the whole bottle. By my standards, given my history, it definitely felt addictive and excessive.

In the course of the next few years, I "decided" several times to stop drinking completely, but before long, I'd start in again. Clearly "I" was not calling the shots. But through it all, awareness was effortlessly beholding the whole thing as it was happening—noticing the urge to drink, how it felt in the body, what thoughts argued for and against drinking, how it felt to buy the bottle, to open it, to pour the first glass, to take the first sip, how I felt after the first glass, what it was that sometimes moved me to have a second glass, how I felt the next morning.

There were some very interesting discoveries during this process. For example, I found that while I totally enjoyed how I felt after one glass of wine, I didn't actually enjoy how I felt as I got drunker, especially if I drank more than two glasses. Nonetheless, on many occasions, something compelled me to keep going, even though I didn't actually enjoy how it made me feel. I went on a number of week-long silent meditation retreats during these years when I was drinking off and on, and I discovered that in the middle of a retreat, when awareness was very clear, not only did the very thought of drinking a glass of wine and blurring my consciousness sound undesirable, but I was actually viscerally *repelled* by the idea. There was an openness, a subtlety, a sensitivity at those times that didn't want to be dulled.

There was a curiosity about all of this and a trust in the process. I had a healthy concern about my drinking, but I never feared that I would be plunged back into the kind of totally out-of-control and wildly destructive drinking I had done decades earlier. I knew with certainty that wasn't where I was headed. I can't explain *how* I knew this, but I did. It's like how I know with doubtless certainty that I'm never going to love eating chopped liver and I'm never going to become a high school math teacher. I just *know*.

After a few years of drinking this way off and on and being effortlessly aware of the whole thing as it happened, a decision emerged not to drink anymore. This decision felt entirely different from all the previous decisions that had failed. It seemed to come not from the thinking mind, not from the part of me that was in conflict with my drinking, but rather from nondual awareness, the unconditional love that has no problem with anything. This was not the dualistic, fear-based desire to stop rooted in the thought that "I" was in trouble and needed fixing. This came from an absence of conflict and separation. There was a felt difference that I cannot entirely articulate, but the hallmark of it was a certainty, an absence of doubt that I could never have manufactured or engineered. It was exactly the same kind of experience I'd had back in 1973 when I first sobered up. I *knew* beyond the shadow of a doubt when I met my therapist for the first time that something had completely changed. It was different from all the times when I had tried to stop before and failed. I *knew* I wasn't going back. No one can manufacture this kind of certainty or *make* this kind of shift happen. On both occasions, it was clearly not my doing.

The therapist with whom I sobered up years ago called sobriety a choice. She believed the person had the power, not the substance. AA, on the other hand, prescribes a path to recovery that begins with admitting that we are powerless over the substance and that only a power greater than ourselves can save us. My therapist believed that complete, permanent abstinence was not necessary. AA believes it absolutely is. These are two different models, different maps, different sets of instructions, but they both point to the same freedom from addiction. They just conceptualize it and get to it in different ways. No one is in control of what map we're drawn to, or which one we stumble upon, or which one works for us. And in the end, we don't *really* know why we started drinking or how we stopped or how or why *anything* happens. The stories of cause and effect are only stories made-up after the fact.

Like many people, I have *seemingly* made a choice to abstain from smoking and drinking. But what inspired and enabled me to make these "choices" when I did? Why did it work when it did and not on previous attempts that had failed? What shifted when the decision felt like it came from nondual awareness and had that doubtless certainty about it? What allows me to stick with these choices in any given moment of temptation? Why was I sometimes able to have one glass of wine and sometimes unable to resist pouring myself a second? If we look deeply, we find no single cause, no easy explanation. If anything, there is an infinite and untraceable web of causes and conditions. Does it follow that because I and many others have successfully stopped drinking and smoking that therefore anyone else can do the same thing? I might have thought so had it not been for the fingerbiting compulsion I have struggled with since childhood.

I have "made a decision" more times than I can count to stop biting my fingers, but as of this writing, in spite of my best efforts, it hasn't worked for longer than a few months at most. Sooner or later, at least so far, the compulsion or what drives it seems to over-power the desire and the intention not to do it. I've tried every imaginable cure, and so far, the compulsion always comes back. Of course, most of the time during any ordinary day, the urge to do this is absent, otherwise I would bite my fingers continuously, which I don't. Most of the time, the very thought of biting my fingers sounds painful and unappealing. In the last year, several times out of the blue, quite mysteriously, the whole compulsion has fallen away by itself for a whole month or more without my intending or trying to stop—it just simply *disappears* and is totally absent. At these times, it's not that I'm *resisting* the urge—the urge is completely *gone*. The compulsion is simply *not there* anymore. This is quite mind-blowing and wonderful when it happens unbidden for a whole month of more. I get very hopeful. But then so far, just as mysteriously, one day out of the blue for no discernable reason, it all comes back. The over-powering urge returns, the impossibility of resisting the urge, the compulsive biting, the inability to stop, the whole thing is suddenly back in full force. Even if it doesn't come back this time, I've had plenty of experiences where it did.

My experiences with this fingerbiting compulsion have given me a deep and irrefutable insight into the compulsory nature of life, the way it all happens by itself. The notion that I can somehow willfully decide or intentionally choose to stop the biting has popped up again and again. I "decide" to stop. I take vows. I really mean it. I pray, I meditate, I do everything in my power to not bite my fingers. And again and again, this notion that I have control has been shot down. In spite of my best efforts not to do so, I find myself again compelled to bite my fingers. My vow fails. But like a boxer who refuses to go down for the final count, I get up and try again. I renew my vow. Again and again, I am knocked down, and again and again, I get up and try again. And "I" don't do this. Life moves through this ever-changing form called Joan in whatever ways it does, taking vows and breaking them, biting my fingers and not biting them. On the surface, this compulsion seems like a form of suffering, a misfortune, an obstacle. And in many ways it certainly has been. But it has also given me an insight into the nature of life that I might not have gotten in any other way.

I understand from my experience with fingerbiting how it is that some people can sober up and stay sober while other people can't, or why some people can't stop themselves from doing terrible things like molesting small children or committing serial murders. We *seem* to have a choice when our action matches our initial intention, but often, it doesn't turn out that way. In one moment, we want to stop smoking and in the next moment, we want a cigarette more than we want to stop. Can we choose what we want or which desire wins out in any given moment? Why do some people have an over-powering compulsion to plan a genocide, while most of us feel no such urge? Why do some people seem to have more will-power or better impulse-control than others? Is all of that a choice?

More and more, brain science is revealing that many of the things we have long considered to be psychological, spiritual or moral strengths and weaknesses are in fact the result of genetics, neurology, hormonal and neuro-chemical changes, problems with the endocrine system, undetected brain conditions, and a host of other factors including diet, early childhood experiences, socioeco-nomic conditions, our moment in history, post-traumatic stress, exposure to electromagnetic fields or toxic chemi-cals, and all kinds of seemingly random things that you would never imagine might be having an impact on your "choices" about something such as fingerbiting or smok-ing. For example, the shape of your throat and your air-way may lead to undiagnosed sleep disorders that have recently been linked to such things as depression and attention deficit disorder, and those in turn might trigger a desire to engage in some kind of comforting, addictive, self-soothing behavior.

We judge ourselves so harshly for being the way we are—for not making enough money, for not being neat enough, for eating too much, for being too fat, for not going to the gym enough, for getting angry, for not being a better mother or a better daughter or a better husband, for not being able to stop smoking, for being depressed, for not being able to snap out of it, for not being present or "in the now" enough, for thinking and daydreaming too much, and on and on—as if there were some single entity called "me" inside this bodymind who could and should get it together and do a better job of steering the ship.

But no such entity can actually be found. One neuroscientist has recently compared the brain to a "team of rivals," and much of what drives us is below the level of conscious awareness. No one is in control—not God, not Zeus, not "me." Those are all mythological characters (unless we understand God in a very different way).

And yet, if we are hurting ourselves and others, there is a natural desire to find a way to stop. This desire is the movement of life itself, as is the apparent process of going into a recovery program, taking up a meditation practice, doing a Feldenkrais lesson, studying yoga, attending talks on radical nonduality, or whatever life moves us to do. Sometimes, the cure works. When the right conditions come together, sobering up happens, or waking up from the dream of being a separate person happens, or being able to meet hatred with love happens, or dissolving into boundless presence happens. When other conditions come together, getting drunk happens, or believing in the mirage of separation and encapsulation happens, or meeting hatred with hatred happens, or being totally hypnotized by thoughts and ideas happens. It all happens to no one. No one is in control of what remedies we are moved to try and what outcomes they seem to bring about. When we *see* how choiceless it all is, there is compassion for ourselves and others when it doesn't all go the way we *think* it should.

It has been a huge relief to really *see* that there is no central executive who chooses what things to do or what outcomes will result from what is done, and to really get how impersonal our inner weather systems are. Some bodyminds have more stormy weather than other bodyminds, just as some geographical locations have more stormy weather than others, and it is neither helpful nor relevant to compare ourselves to others. It is also very liberating to realize that change always happens on its own timetable, not on the timetable the thinking mind conjures up. Especially in our speeded-up, fast-food, modern culture, we tend to want instant results, and life just doesn't work that way. Most changes in nature happen slowly.

Whenever this bodymind character called Joan seems like an actual, solid entity, when I identify this character as who I am, when the stories about "Joan the Neurotic Fingerbiter" seem believable and true, there is suffering. The actual physical pain of biting my fingers pales in comparison to this psychological pain. But when there is a waking up from all of these thoughts and stories and a recognition of the bigger picture, the awareness beholding it all, the boundlessness of being, then all of this psychological suffering melts away.

Over time, this fingerbiting compulsion has diminished in intensity. It happens less frequently and less severely when it does, and it disappears for longer periods of time. But perhaps more importantly, I no longer feel ashamed of this compulsion. I am willing for it to be with me to the end of my life if that's what happens. Of course, I would like it to go away, and I hope it does. But I used to feel tortured by this compulsion and by my inability to control it. I believed all the stories in my mind about what this compulsion meant about me, that I was an unenlightened loser and that if only I would do a better job of "being aware" and "being in the now" more of the time, this obviously wouldn't be happening. It is a great relief to no longer believe these stories. They still show up from time to time, and occasionally they still take hold and momentarily seem believable, but the hypnotic spell doesn't last very long. It quickly becomes obvious that these stories and the character at the center of them are all a creation of smoke and mirrors.

I've experienced first-hand *both* the relief of recognizing that there is no one in control *and* the relative value of such things as therapy, meditation, martial arts training and somatic awareness work in opening up new possibilities. I've seen how the bodymind—the brain and the nervous system—can learn new ways of functioning. In addition to uncovering many previously unsuspected causes for behaviors previously considered to be spiritual or moral weaknesses, brain science has also discovered that the brain has great plasticity—it can change in ways we never imagined before. Of course, no independent agent is in control of any of this change. We don't learn these new ways of functioning on command by some act of will. In fact, much of this learning and transformation happens outside of conscious awareness. But learning *does* happen (*when the necessary conditions come together*). So radical nonduality doesn't mean we have to renounce all such activities. It simply means they are a causeless happening of the whole universe. Nonduality recognizes that there is nothing we need to do (other than exactly what we are doing), but it doesn't tell us that we need to do nothing. There is a big difference.

We can speak of these activities in the language of choice and responsibility, or we can speak of them in the language of choiceless happenings, but these are simply different ways of describing or conceptualizing the same events, different maps of the same territory. As always, what really matters is the territory, not the map. It's fine to use the map, but we go astray when we confuse it with the territory or insist that it is the One True Map.

Dogmatic nondualism is an oxymoron, so whenever we notice ourselves getting fixated on any particular conceptual ideology, model or map, perhaps it will prompt us to wonder anew what it is that we know with absolute certainty. This question brings us quickly back to the non-conceptual bare actuality Here / Now that cannot be formulated.

The mind always wants to pin things down, get a grip, find solid ground on which to stand. It has endless ideas about how everything is and what "I" should do to improve myself and get somewhere better than where I am.

If we're lucky, we begin to see that the thinking mind is not in the driver's seat and never has been, that the "I" it pretends to be is only a kind of thought-image superimposed on our actual present moment experiencing, that we're not going anywhere, for we are always Here / Now. And if we're lucky, we begin to get more interested in Here / Now than in our thoughts, memories and fantasies about someplace else (including our thoughts about how to *get* Here / Now *in the future*). If we're lucky, we find ourselves more interested in the groundlessness of actual direct experiencing than in the hopeless project of trying to get a grip on the inexplicable and ever-changing happening of life. We stop trying to formulate life into an ideology we can hold onto, and we dissolve instead into simply *being* life, just as it is.

Wherever we go, here we always are, and we can always trust that life is unfolding in exactly the way it is.

Thoughts about "what if" and "if only" and "I'm not there yet" and "this isn't it" and "this shouldn't be the way it is" make us miserable. We can't "decide" not to think these kinds of thoughts. That doesn't work. But we may find that simply *seeing* how this kind of seeking and grasping and "arguing with reality" happens gradually erodes these habits and tendencies of mind. By simply *seeing* this mental exertion (again and again) as it happens and recognizing it as a form of suffering, naturally, these habits begin to drop away.

But don't expect them to fall away all at once, permanently, in the way we'd like them to when we imagine "The Perfect Me" or "The Pain-Free Life"—that very expectation is just more seeking, more "if only." Life happens as it happens. And for most of us, there is no end to the ways these old habitual movements of the mind can show up. There is no end to waking up, just as there is no end to Here/Now. And whether there is seeking or relaxing, contracting or expanding, thinking or not-thinking, fingerbiting or no fingerbiting, it's all part of the dance.

Awareness

Right now, there is the seamless immediacy of breathing, awaring, sensing, thinking, being—the sounds of traffic, the warm breeze, the dancing shadows on the wall, the movement of fingers on the keyboard—the utter simplicity of this present happening. There is nothing confusing about the present moment until we begin thinking about it. We can conceptually divide up this seamless happening with words, but what we're creating by doing that is only a map. *The territory itself is always seamless.* I keep mentioning this because it's easy to forget, and because I'm about to embark on some map-making.

In various books and talks about nonduality, the words awareness and consciousness get used in a variety of different ways by different authors and often by the same author in different moments. This can be confusing, and it's helpful to remember that the confusion is always in the map and not in the territory.

I use the word consciousness to refer to the movie of waking life, everything perceivable and conceivable, this whole phenomenal appearance. I use the word awareness in two different ways, as either the all-pervasive ground of being or else as the light behind attention. It's the same awareness in each case, just a different aspect of it that is being highlighted. Attention, as I use the word, refers to a particular focus of awareness, paying attention to something in particular, whereas awareness has no focus and no object. Awareness beholds and includes everything. It is another word for Here / Now. Thought is the mental process that reflects on what appears in awareness—labeling, classifying, dividing, speculating, strategizing, and analyzing what appears. Consciousness creates diversity and variety, but consciousness without thought (bare perception) is seamless and immediate. It takes thinking to create the *idea* of separation, division and conflict. Thought deals in concepts, abstractions and models. It is inherently dualistic and representational. Awareness, on the other hand, is nonconceptual, holistic, immediate and direct (unmediated).

Awareness is present *prior* to consciousness, attention, and thought; it is present *during* consciousness, attention, and thought; and it is present *after* consciousness, attention, and thought. Neither consciousness, attention, nor thought can appear without awareness, but awareness does not depend in any way on consciousness, attention, or thought in order to be. Awareness is what *sees* thinking and *recognizes* a thought as a thought. It is what knows consciousness. It is the light behind attention. It is what attention *is*. Consciousness, attention, and thought all come and go. Awareness is what beholds it all. Awareness has no qualities of its own.

As the all-pervasive ground of being or the Ultimate Subject, awareness has no opposite and no other. It is the water in every wave, and it is that which remains when everything perceivable and conceivable disappears. In this sense, awareness never comes or goes, and never increases or decreases, for it is all there is.

Some authors use the word Consciousness in this same absolute sense, and some authors don't use either consciousness or awareness to stand for Ultimate Reality. Some authors say that awareness is the first appearance, the first manifestation (or imagination) that comes and goes. And indeed, every night in deep sleep, the first, bare *sense* of awareness disappears, and the *thought* of awareness disappears, and all these words disappear, and the one who cares about figuring all this out disappears. What remains is actually unnamable. By definition, it is nothing perceivable or conceivable. Whether we call it primordial awareness, the Ultimate Subject, Ultimate Reality, the Absolute, the Self, Consciousness, unicity, or blipity-bloop doesn't really matter as long as we understand how we are using the words.

Whatever we call this unnamable absolute, it is not an object. It doesn't exist as "something" apart from everything else, for it is that which has no opposite and no other. It is the emptiness of everything, the no-*thing*-ness, the ungraspable formlessness. It shows up *as* awareness, *as* consciousness, *as* thinking, *as* waking and dreaming, *as* deep sleep, *as* the sense of being a person and *as* the sense of being boundless impersonal presence. It is the timelessness and spacelessness that appears as time and space. It *is* everything, but it is nothing in particular. It is equally and completely present everyplace and everywhen. Anything we can name (consciousness, awareness, the Ultimate Subject, the Self, the Absolute) inevitably sounds like *something* once we have a word for it, but we can never actually pin down what it is we are talking about. As with any "thing" the mind tries to grasp, when we look closely, nothing is there (apart from everything).

When people speak of "awareness practices" or awareness as a key to liberation, the word awareness is being used to point to the power behind attention. It is in this sense that people speak of cultivating awareness or being more or less aware in different moments. In this sense of the word, awareness is the central ingredient in insight meditation, nonconceptual inquiry, intelligent psychotherapy and somatic practices such as Feldenkrais. It is the intelligence that sheds light and dissolves illusion.

When we speak of awareness as the light behind attention, it's important to recognize that the thinking mind (posing as "me") doesn't control this power. Awareness is upstream from that movement of thought that pretends to be the author of my life. So although we *seem* to have some control over where we place our attention, we can't really manipulate awareness at will or "use" it for the purposes that thought conjures up. We can only dissolve into awareness or *be* awareness. And while we can't *not* be awareness in the bigger sense of the word, we *can* be unaware in this more limited sense of the word. We can be inattentive, distracted, mindless or ignore-ant. Awareness practices are about becoming more attentive, more mindful, more present, more awake to what is.

That may sound like self-improvement, but paradoxically, awareness by its very nature doesn't need anything to be other than exactly how it is. It doesn't go to war with the way things are, it simply exposes them to the light. It allows everything to undo itself. Awareness is unconditional love, absolute devotion. It accepts everything.

I talked before about how awareness helped to dissolve my addiction to drinking, how there was a natural awareness of the whole process as it was happening until eventually a decision to stop emerged spontaneously from life itself. You could see in that example that awareness works at its own speed, that it cannot be manipulated by "me," that many other forces of nature and nurture played a part in what unfolded and that ultimately, no one really knows why I stopped drinking.

Bringing awareness (or attention) to various places in the body, or to different patterns of thought and behavior, is like turning on a light in a previously darkened room. Things are revealed, clarified and dissolved. But if we try to "use" this wonderful power to get a certain outcome, and especially if we want instant, dramatic and permanent results, usually we are disappointed. It *can* happen that an old habit will dissolve instantly and permanently in one great flash of light, never to return ever again, but more often, this is not the case. And even when something *does* seem to completely and permanently disappear, even then, as my experience with drinking shows, we never know when it might come back. Ultimately, we discover it doesn't really matter whether an old habit shows up again or not, including the habit of identifying as the bodymind and feeling encapsulated as the character. All such experiences are seen to be momentary, dream-like appearances arising in awareness, including the "me" who claims to be the owner of these experiences. There is less and less preoccupation with improving, fixing and perfecting this imaginary "me," who is seen to be only a mirage. That doesn't mean we no longer have any interest in healing what is broken or clearing up what is murky and confused, but our interest is coming from love instead of from fear. We aren't opposing the way life is, trying to escape from it, or seeking a personal result to make "me" special.

If we get caught up in seeking that kind of special achievement, or if we begin imagining that "I" am now enlightened and beyond it all, that very idea is instant delusion and a new self-image to protect and defend. Awareness *reveals* these kinds of delusions; it exposes them to the light.

Many people devote their lives to cultivating awareness in one way or another, and this is beautiful. Ultimately, awareness is the great dissolver. It dissolves boundaries and limitations, it dissolves suffering, it dissolves every fixation. It leaves only the groundless ground, the openness that allows everything and sticks to nothing.

Attention is always limited and temporary. The lens of attention moves from one focus to the next in the same way that everything else in the universe happens. No individual is pulling the strings. The urge and the "decision" to pay attention to my left foot in any given moment comes out of infinite causes and conditions, and the ability to do this depends on the condition of the brain and body. But we're more than this conditioned appearance, so waking up is always a balance between the recognition that everything *within* the appearance is a choiceless, conditioned happening, and at the same time, the discovery of the unconditioned, causeless awareness (the boundless love, the Open Heart, the undivided energy, the infinite potential) that is our True Nature.

Because awareness dissolves illusion so completely, some teachers who focus on cultivating awareness think that it can solve every problem. Many people believe that enlightenment will magically erase every human blemish, that if we meditate enough or have an awakening to our True Nature, then problems such as depression, anxiety or addiction will all fall away forever and we will live happily ever after. And if that doesn't happen, if these problems keep showing up, then we feel like a failure.

Or we think that the guru is a fraud because he still has human weaknesses and imperfections.

In fact, there are many biological, chemical, neurological, psychological, medical or social conditions that cannot be solved by awareness alone, and enlightenment does not mean that all of these problems are suddenly fixed. Enlightenment simply *sees* that all conditions and expressions of life are an impersonal appearance with no enduring substance. It sees them with compassion and boundless love. It sees the light in the darkness. And it also doesn't hide in the light to avoid the darkness.

Wholeness includes everything, the light and the dark. In nature, there are many false starts, many discards, many individuals who die young or never fully develop. Some flowers freeze before they ever get to blossom. Some waves fizzle out while others tower and roll magnificently, but it's one ocean doing it all. It's all part of the natural process. Fizzling out prematurely or never getting to blossom sounds tragic and terribly unfair if we're identified as a separate fragment, but from the perspective of the whole, it's all part of the dance.

When it is realized that every moment is empty of self, then everything is allowed to happen in its own way, at its own speed, as it does anyway. The whole *effort* to "be here now" falls away along with the one who needs anything to be different from exactly how it is. We wake up to the luminous, vibrant aliveness that is manifesting as the sounds of rain and traffic, the taste of tea, the cool breeze, the green leaves sparkling in the sunlight and dancing in the wind, the white clouds blowing across the blue sky, the red fire truck streaking past, siren wailing. This is the extraordinary miracle of ordinary life. It is always available, but only ever here and now.

The kind of transformation through awareness that I have been describing may happen in the context of formal meditation or some other spiritual practice in a traditional setting, it may happen through reading books on radical nonduality that tell you again and again that "this is it, just as it is," it may happen through some kind of somatic movement or energy work, it may happen on its own in a totally informal way. It may not happen at all on a level where the rational, cognitive mind can understand it or put it into words. The intelligence of awareness, or of life itself, operates at a level that is deeper than or beyond the cognitive mind.

One contemporary Zen teacher even goes so far as to say that clarity is overrated. He feels pre-dawn zazen (sitting meditation) is powerful precisely because you are still half asleep in that liminal place where the unconscious dreaming mind and the vacancy of deep sleep are still very much present. And I'm guessing that some people may be getting the same results by staying in bed! In fact, in Feldenkrais training, if you fell asleep during class, this was looked upon as part of the process and was never discouraged. It was recognized that the brain and nervous system were absorbing and processing new information at a different level from conscious wakefulness.

There is no magic formula, no silver bullet for transformation, and ultimately it is recognized that boundlessness is equally present as tension, contraction, dullness, boredom, depression, anxiety, restlessness, agitation, anger, worry, upset, addiction, and all other forms of overcast, cloudy, turbulent or stormy weather. Nothing is left out. Waking up is not a perpetually sunny day. But when there is a shift from being caught up in thought to being fully present as open awareness, suffering ends. We begin to discover that our apparent problem, our suffering, can only be resolved *now,* not yesterday or tomorrow or once-and-for-all, but only now.

Past and future only exist as thought-forms or as memories and imaginations appearing Here / Now. But awareness is nonconceptual, timeless and immediate. It is what Here / Now *is.*

Words are only pointers. In reality, there is no separation between thinking and awaring, or between consciousness and awareness, or between awareness and Ultimate Reality, or between form and emptiness, or between deep sleep and the movie of waking life, or between samsara and nirvana. *These are many words for one happening. The words only seem to divide what is actually undivided.* In the end, the words are all "sound and fury, signifying nothing."

When we wake up from the confusion of words, from the mental maps and the stories about how everything works, the stories of cause and effect, progress and regress—when we wake up from all of that sound and fury, we realize the undivided simplicity of what is. This bare being is at once obvious, unavoidable and completely inconceivable. It cannot be explained or understood, formulated or figured out. We cannot grasp it, nor can we reject it. This is it, right here, right now, just as it is.

Is There *Anything* to Do?

Realization is nothing to be gained anew...
Realization consists of getting rid of the false idea
that one is not realized.

—Ramana Maharshi

Once you understand that the false needs time and
what needs time is false, you are nearer the Reality,
which is timeless, ever in the now.... *If you need*
time to achieve something, it must be false. The real
is always with you; you need not wait to be what
you are. Only you must not allow your mind to go
out of yourself in search.

—Nisargadatta Maharaj

The question is not what should I do in the future to
get it, but, rather, what am I presently doing that
prevents me from realizing it right now?

—Alan Watts

When we maintain awareness, whether we know
it or not, healing is taking place... a door that has
been shut begins to open.... As the door opens, we
see that the present is absolute and that, in a sense,
the whole universe begins right now, in each second.
And the healing of life is in that second of simple

awareness.... Healing is always just being here,
with a simple mind.

—Charlotte Joko Beck

Choice implies consciousness—a high degree of
consciousness. Without it, you have no choice.
Choice begins the moment you disidentify from the
mind and its conditioned patterns, the moment you
become present. Until you reach that point, you
are unconscious, spiritually speaking. This means
you are compelled to think, feel, and act in certain
ways according to the conditioning of your mind....
Presence is the key. The Now is the key.

—Eckhart Tolle

In simple presence with what is right here now, be it
joyful or painful, an amazing freedom reveals itself.
It cannot be described or explained in words. It is
the freedom to be totally, effortlessly the way things
are at this moment.

—Toni Packer

When people hear the radical nondual message that everything is a choiceless happening and that there is no
self and nothing to attain, they often think this means
that they "shouldn't" meditate or do yoga or practice to
improve their tennis game. In fact, what this nondual
message points to is that any of this may indeed happen, but that there is never any independent executive
doing it. There is *never* a thinker behind the thoughts or
an actor behind the action. The separate person we *seem*

to be is only an appearance, a mental image, a story, a concept, a mirage. Our actual *experience*, if we pay attention to it, is boundless and seamless, ever-changing and ever-present, utterly immediate and without separation. Everything that happens is the undivided movement of life itself.

In the movie-story of waking life, we may indeed recover from an addiction, learn to handle stress in a better way, or experience a profound awakening, but *none* of this—if it happens—is the result of individual free will, although it may *seem* to be, and there is no one at the center of these events who is being improved by them, for no such separate, persisting entity actually exists. Our whole spiritual adventure, all the magnificent awakening experiences and all the moments of apparent backsliding, are a kind of dream-like appearance. The forms that appear may *seem* solid and real at first glance, but look more closely, and the whole show turns out to be no more solid than ripples on a pond or smoke curling into the air.

Activities such as meditation, yoga or psychotherapy may appear to be helpful within the movie of waking life, although of course any story we formulate about cause and effect or improvement is a conceptual overlay. But with that caveat in mind, I can say that I've experienced in my own life the transformative power of various forms of awareness work including meditation, inquiry, Feldenkrais, and psychotherapy, and I've also experienced the liberating effects of books and meetings about radical nonduality. All of these happenings seem to have played a part in *seeing through* the imaginary problem, *seeing* how suffering was being created and sustained, waking up from the dream-like "story of my life," and discovering the simplicity of bare presence and the freedom of needing nothing other than what is.

Does that mean that these activities *caused* this insight or this bare presence or this freedom, or that they are the essential prescription that everyone else needs to follow to get the same results? No, it just means that in my experience, this is what happened. And even then, it is all a story, a mental construction after the fact. Nothing has really happened. Here / Now is uncaused. It is not a result of anything else. Wherever we go, we never get any closer to Here / Now. Whatever changes happen to the waves, they are never any more or less the ocean. Changes can happen, but they only make a *relative* difference, *in* the movie-story of waking life. When we wake up from a dream, the dream-problem and the dream-solution both disappear. The whole thing was make-believe.

There is no way to *become* what we already are and what already is. If things like meditation, or satsang, or books like this one, or meetings on radical nonduality have any usefulness, it is in exposing the illusion that something is lacking, that there is time in which to attain something, and that there is *somebody* who needs to be transformed. But by their very nature, intentional activities or practices cannot help but reinforce these illusions to some degree (and that includes the non-practice of radical nonduality as soon as we formalize it by writing a book or holding a meeting), so people have sometimes compared all such happenings and practices to fighting fire with fire or selling water by the banks of the river.

To simply adopt the *idea* that "All is One," that there is "no self," that "everything is perfect as it is" as a philosophy or a belief probably won't resolve the fundamental unease and longing that prompts the spiritual quest in the first place. Belief is always shadowed by doubt and tends to crumble when the waters get rough. And so, as long as delusion and suffering continue to show up, practice in some form will probably continue to show up as well, whether it is the practice of drinking alcohol, the practice of compulsive shopping, the practice of meditation (formally or spontaneously), or the practice of going to hear nondual teachers who tell you there is no one to practice. Such things as meditation, satsang, and meetings about nonduality are ways of exposing the imaginary nature of the problem and revealing the nondual boundlessness that has never been absent.

To reveal what is obvious, unavoidable, and never-not-here requires an approach that is not result-oriented, an approach that goes nowhere, an approach that is utterly useless and without purpose. Such an approach begins with the recognition that there is no one to be enlightened and that any so-called enlightenment is *in* the dream-like movie, and therefore, whether there is enlightenment or delusion in any given moment doesn't actually matter at all, for it's all part of the show and none of it is personal.

Of course, practically speaking, in everyday life, it makes a huge difference whether we are suffering or free from suffering. Thus, practices and non-practices tend to keep showing up, and they are as much an act of nature as the wind and the tides and the rotation of the planets.

Basic awareness meditation is really nothing more or less than giving open, nonjudgmental attention to present-moment, non-conceptual experiencing. You don't have to be in the lotus position. This can happen on the city bus. That enjoyment of bare being and thoughtless presence dissolves the imaginary problem and reveals the boundlessness that has no center. Without *some* kind of nonconceptual exploration of this kind, it's easy for us to get stuck in *thinking* about all of this and trying to resolve it intellectually through analytical thinking and philosophizing. That tends to result in frustration—chasing the proverbial carrot on the never-ending treadmill—and it often leads to picking up new beliefs and dogmas—the dogma of nonduality. But true nonduality is not a belief or a dogma. It is the ever-present, ever-changing, totally immediate and unavoidable actuality that is effortlessly presenting itself right now.

Of course, once "meditation" becomes something special, something we're *trying* to do, then it can easily become an obstacle. We approach it with a goal-oriented, dualistic mindset. We strive to be good meditators and feel alternately proud and deflated as we seem to succeed or fail at whatever it is we imagine we are supposed to be doing. We may think that our goal is to stop thinking, or that our goal is to be calm and full of love and joy. We get caught up in trying to repeat experiences of clarity or bliss, and we strive for some monumental breakthrough, some imaginary awakening. We get the idea that meditation is spiritual and watching television is not. This is where radical nonduality can provide a wonderful knock-out punch.

Of course, the mind hears that and immediately imagines a final event—a decisive blow, an explosive transformation, a finish-line that "I" can finally cross. Whereas the knock-out is actually the realization that there is no one to be knocked out and no finish-line to cross. The problem we are trying to solve never actually existed.

So, there *are* things to do, or more accurately, there are things that may happen, but no one is doing them.

And yet, if we think we are being passively swept along by some force outside of us, that isn't really on the mark either. It's more like, nothing is being swept along because all there is, is seamless movement, and we are that.

And *as* that seamless movement of life, there is an undeniable ability right here to open and close my hand apparently "at will," and to deny this ability would be absurd. And yet, I cannot find any entity who is initiating, authoring, controlling or doing this action, nor can I tell you how "I" do this. The impulse to open my hand in any given moment comes from the whole universe, as do the ten million things that make this action possible (brain, nerves, muscles, bones, water, air, sunlight, and so on). There is nothing confusing about the actual event of opening and closing my hand. The confusion comes when I begin to *think* about this action and try to formulate some abstract metaphysical position about free will or the self. Then suddenly this simple action gets very confusing and paradoxical. It seems confusing and paradoxical only because words and concepts can't ever capture the actuality.

When the right conditions come together, the bodymind *can* learn or be trained in all kinds of ways so that it has more choices, better choices, more control, more refined control, more possibilities, or however we want to put it. A skilled athlete has more choices, more control, more possibilities for how to move her body than someone without that training and practice. Spiritual teachings that offer something to do function in much the same manner as athletic training. Such teachings speak *to* that ability Here / Now to act, to formulate intentions, to make choices, to push through obstacles, to persevere.

While most mainstream versions of the great spiritual traditions usually do assume the existence of free will, and do address themselves to the illusory separate self, and are very dualistic in their outlook, it is also possible to speak to that ability Here / Now from a non-conceptual, nondual perspective, without in any way presuming the reality of a separate self with free will. The clearest teachings, traditional or nontraditional, *do* see through the illusory self, but they also recognize the ability Here / Now to act, and they know that this capacity, this response-ability, can potentially—when the right conditions come together—be cultivated and refined in much the same way that an athlete or an artist can develop their skills through practice.

Of course, *all* of that training, practice, ability and perseverance happens out of infinite causes and conditions and could not be otherwise in any moment than exactly how it is. No independent executive is "doing" any of this. It is the activity of life itself. Nevertheless, it *can* happen *when the right conditions come together.* And you (this aware presence that is Here / Now) *are* life itself. So although there is no choice in one sense, you still (when life so moves you) have to cook dinner, get a job, practice the piano, take up meditation, go into a recovery program, train for the Olympics, shoot heroin or whatever happens through this character. You don't just sit motionlessly on the couch "doing nothing," hoping that food will magically finds its way into your mouth. There is a power *right here* that acts and *you are that*. You earn a living, shop for groceries, cook dinner, bring the food from the plate to your mouth and chew it. It is all the flow of life happening effortlessly by itself in the only possible way, and yet, experientially, *you* are doing it, although if "you" observe closely, no discrete "you" *apart* from this happening can ever actually be found.

This power that acts is not the phantom "me," the imaginary executive, which is only a mirage. Nor is it the thinking mind which only *pretends* to be in control and which takes credit after the fact. The source of all action is prior to thought and prior to any imaginary executive that we think is running the show. We all *experience* this power, this source, directly. It is Here / Now reading these words. How could "I" (or anything) be *other* than this creative power, this universal intelligence, this primordial energy, this aware presence? This is truly all there is.

Although everything is one, undivided, seamless energy, at the same time, apples are not oranges. Neuroscience has shown that different actions involve different parts of the brain, and experientially we can all discern a palpable difference between action that flows spontaneously from nondual presence or unclouded awareness (being "in the zone" or "in the now") in contrast to action that is somehow inhibited or tripped-up by dualistic thought patterns such as doubt, hesitation and second-guessing ourselves. Everything is one reality *and* we can identify different aspects of that reality. Both sides of the equation are true. Not one, not two.

When we are caught up in the hypnotic entrancement of obsessive, dysfunctional, self-centered thinking, we feel tight, contracted, rigid and trapped. We feel separate. The discovery that liberates us is not a philosophy or a belief. It is the dissolution of the imaginary problem in the openness of Here / Now.

When consciousness can relax into the simplicity of bare presence, something opens up. We are in harmony with a greater intelligence, or more accurately, the illusion that we are separate from this falls away. This is what Leonard Cohen pointed to when he said, "You abandon your masterpiece and you sink into the real Masterpiece." You give up trying to control life or trying to *think* your way to liberation, and you relax into what you already are and cannot *not* be, this ever-present, all-inclusive immediacy that is happening effortlessly by itself.

Who or what is it that can shift from the tightness and encapsulation of thought to the openness of clear awareness and nonconceptual being? The same intelligence that learns how to walk, how to ride a bicycle, how to swim, how to read these words. It happens by itself through this capacity right here to act. There is no "actor" behind the action. It is a happening of life itself. No one can really explain how this shift happens—life finds its way into it in much the same way that life discovers how to ride a bicycle or how to swim. You would be hard-pressed to describe how "you" do either of those things or to write up a set of instructions for anyone else to follow that would tell them how to ride a bicycle or how to swim, and yet, these abilities can be discovered.

In a similar way, we can discover what it means to make no effort, to relax into the groundlessness of Here / Now, to open the Heart, to simply *be*. None of this happens on command by an act of will. It is the falling away of this kind of result-oriented exertion, and it is the falling away of any belief that we are in control, that we are running the show. And depending upon the weather conditions of a particular moment and a particular bodymind organism, this ability to relax the thinking mind, to see through the imaginary problem and wake up to the simplicity of the present moment may be more or less difficult to access. Sometimes, that ability to relax is not available, and when it isn't, don't take it personally. And when it *is* available, don't take that personally either! Whether there is relaxing or tensing-up, all of this is a choiceless happening of the whole universe. Ultimately, there is nothing to give up and nothing that needs relaxing.

Perhaps a more helpful question than "What *should* I do?" is "What *am* I doing?" Asking what we "should" do invites thinking, and specifically, thinking about the imaginary future. Whereas "What am I doing?" invites awareness, awareness of the present moment, as it is. Instead of being lost in a mental realm of imaginary possibilities and "shoulds," our attention comes back to the bare sensations and movements of this moment. And in this bare actuality, there is no problem, no self, no separation.

Am I saying we shouldn't think? Of course not. Thinking is part of what the universe is doing. Thinking happens by itself—we don't really know in advance what our next thought will be—"the thinker" who seems to be authoring our thoughts is itself a thought, a mental image. Some of our thinking is useful and functional, but we can notice that much of our thinking, maybe most of it, does nothing but generate suffering and confusion. With awareness, we can begin to *feel* when thought ceases to be useful, when it slides over into obsessive rumination. The more we pay attention with awareness to any thought process, the more we can become sensitive to where it ceases to be functional. Ultimately, the clearest and most truly creative decisions, discoveries and breakthroughs come from a place totally beyond the thinking mind. Clarity arrives when thought gets out of the way, and suddenly, with absolute certainty, immediately we *know* what to do, or we *see* the solution to the problem. I'm guessing everyone has experienced this.

When action arises out of unclouded aware presence, which could also be described as the absence (or transparency) of any imagined separation from the seamlessness of being, when that happens, a whole new possibility opens up. In that moment, addiction vanishes, hate dissolves into love, old arguments end, and nothing has to continue in the direction it was going before. There is no resistance to anything. This is an immediate, palpable, experiential reality when it happens, not an ideology or a belief.

We are seemingly bound by conditioning, by the infinite web of cause and effect, nature and nurture. But when we recognize that no-thing actually exists (or stands apart) as we think it does, then what remains to be bound or free?

When an athlete is truly "in the zone," they are totally surrendered, at one with the whole universe. They *are* the Masterpiece. There is no hesitation, no self-concern, no second-guessing, no doubt, no holding back, no resistance, no separation. If you've experienced this, you know what I mean. And you can see it happening in great athletes. For other animals, this is their natural way of being. Only humans have enough brain-power to lose touch with this effortlessness and get tied into knots by thinking about everything. Because we get mixed up in this way, we have such things as meditation, satsang, yoga, Feldenkrais, psychotherapy and nondual teachings to undo the knots and wake us up from our confusion. *We* don't create these things any more than we create our brains, our bodies or our confusion; these things are *all* the activity of life itself.

Zen practice is often described as learning how to be "in the zone" or "in the Now" not just occasionally during an athletic event or on a meditation retreat, but in our whole life. Of course, *all* experiences, including any *experience* of "being in the zone" or "being in the now," are by nature impermanent. They come and go. But it's not really "the Now" or "the Zone" that comes and goes. What comes and goes are the thoughts and stories, the misconceptions that *seem* to obscure the ever-present, all-inclusive ground of being. What I call Here / Now, what is sometimes called primordial awareness, the Ultimate Subject, emptiness, Buddha Nature, the Tao, the Original Face, the One Behind All the Masks, the Self, *this* is never not here. What comes and goes are the ever-changing sensations, perceptions, experiences, thoughts, imaginations and conceptualizations that *appear* Here / Now. So being "in the zone" or "in the Now" is not about acquiring something that is missing, but rather, seeing through what seems to be in the way, relaxing the grasping and seeking movement of mind, letting go into the effortless flow that life is. The words are never quite right, since we are never anything *other* than this effortless flow, so we are always already this. We only *imagine* separation.

Since "the Zone" or "the Now" is actually the ever-present ground of being and not some special thing that we lack and must acquire, this ability to reside in it or wake up to it is a kind of undoing rather than a doing. With awareness, we simply begin to see through the thoughts that tell us "this isn't it," the thoughts that posit a "me" separate from "the Zone," someone who needs to get somewhere other than right here. At the same time, we feel the tightness, the unease of seeking and grasping. As we become aware of how we are holding on, we begin to discover the possibility of relaxing and opening—not striving, not resisting, but simply resting. This resting doesn't mean passivity or inactivity. It might mean running a marathon or climbing a mountain, raising children or building a movement for social justice. But we are discovering how to do whatever we are doing in a restful, effortless way—going with the flow of life rather than fighting against it.

This discovery and learning happens at its own pace, not on the time-table the thinking mind conjures up. Failure is part of the process. It's not about perfection. Sometimes this shift from grasping to relaxing seems to be possible and sometimes it doesn't. We often get the idea that "enlightened people" are permanently established in an expanded state of consciousness, whereas we imagine ourselves to be someone who is flip-flopping in and out of this awakened state. We don't notice that the "someone" who is either "permanently established" or "still flip-flopping" is a fictional creation put together by thought, memory and imagination.

Liberation is waking up from that conceptual picture and recognizing that there is no way out of Here / Now. Liberation doesn't mean being in *any* particular state of consciousness "all the time," for everything perceivable and conceivable is nothing but flux. And the "me" who seems to be having "my experiences" is a mirage, a mental image, a bunch of ever-changing thoughts, memories and stories. So who exactly is having this flip-flop problem? Who is not enlightened?

Even when you're not "in the zone" and you're feeling

separate, this too is nothing but undivided boundlessness appearing to be divided up and separate. So the pathless path is to see, again and again, how we tell the story that "this isn't it," that "I'm not there yet." To wake up is to *see* how confusion and doubt arise, to *see* the misconception, the grasping, the seeking that are presently creating and sustaining this sense of lack, to *see* that the one who seems to have this problem is imaginary, and to see that nothing is left out of the totality, that there is no way to fail.

When we chase after (or try to get rid of) particular experiences or states of mind, we are inevitably frustrated and disappointed. But when we can simply relax into the ever-changing but ever-present obvious, when we realize the thorough-going nature of impermanence, when awareness is awake to its own boundlessness, then we find true freedom and happiness right here, exactly where we are. Here / Now, or the Zone, is our natural state, our True Self. And this True Self is no less fully present if we are biting our fingers, lost in obsessive thoughts or *feeling* tense and separate.

At first, we don't even know what any of this means—"True Self," "Here / Now," "primordial awareness," "aware presence," "undivided being," "presence in the now," "the Masterpiece." If these words are no more than concepts or ideas to you, then you may feel that you don't get it. Of course, you actually *are* experiencing aware presence and undivided being every moment, and there is really nothing *other* than "the Masterpiece," this is what you *are*, this is all there *is*, but you may not *recognize* that yet. At this stage, you're a little bit like Helen Keller before she grokked the word water. You are in the dark. And you have no choice. There is darkness until there isn't.

This sounds dreadful. But again, it only sounds dreadful from the perspective of ignorance. When you *do* finally recognize the simplicity and immediacy of what is, you realize that it was never not here. You realize you were never lost in the first place, that none of what appears Here / Now is personal, neither the ignorance nor the waking up from ignorance. You realize that "you" are not this imaginary little fragment going back and forth between the light and the dark and trying to stay in the light forever, but that you are the whole show. You include absolutely *everything*. You realize that the cloudy, murky, overcast, stormy weather is as much a part of the Masterpiece as the clear, sunny, calm weather.

And when that recognition happens, a possibility opens up that wasn't there before. What do I mean? Let's take an example. When you're a baby, you have to discover how to roll over and how to crawl. You aren't born with the ability to do either of those things. You have the potential ability, but you don't *know* it yet. Before you actually *discover* these abilities for yourself, those possibilities are not available to you. But once you've discovered them, they become increasingly available, and with practice, increasingly easy to access.

In the same way, the possibility of seeing through the imaginary problem, waking up from the hypnotic trance of separation and encapsulation, and simply *being* this present moment, just as it is—shifting from thinking to being—this is a possibility (and in some sense an ability) that is discovered and then in one way or another practiced (formally or informally, consciously or unconsciously), not by "you," but by Life Itself. Over time (and always only now) this new possibility may become increasingly available, increasingly easy to access.

We might say that our practice at this point on the path, once we know firsthand what being awake actually *is*, is to clarify how we move away from the simplicity of Here / Now, how we get lost in confusion, how we do our suffering—to clarify this not by *thinking* about it and analyzing it, but rather, by being *aware* of it as it happens.

I don't mean by this any kind of effortful exertion aimed at self-improvement, and I don't mean any kind of traditional, formal undertaking either. I have nothing against traditional forms, but they are definitely not essential to being awake, and they *can* get in the way if they become a new form of addictive fascination or a new self-improvement project for "me."

However it comes about in different individuals, there is indeed a sensitivity, a capacity for discernment, an ability to let go that can be developed and exercised and honed *when the right conditions come together.* It's just that the source of all this is not the illusory separate "me" and it doesn't *originate* in thought. Thought only describes things after the fact. But there is a an ability to respond that is *right here,* and life—working through you—is discovering and refining this ability.

This discovery and refinement is not something "I" can engineer on command. It's more like awareness spontaneously recognizes that my fist or my heart or my mind is clenched, and in that recognition of the clench, there is suddenly the ability to relax and open. Like falling asleep, it is a letting go. But instead of falling asleep, this is falling awake.

No verbal formulation (choice or no choice, self or no self, practice or no practice) can capture the reality of waking up anymore than we can conceptually capture how swimming, riding a bicycle or reading these words happens. Sometimes this waking up and dissolving happens easily and quickly, sometimes it happens slowly and with many apparent setbacks, sometimes it doesn't happen at all. Life finds its own way with many twists and turns and many apparent mistakes along the way.

Sometimes—often—the power of habit *will* override the ability to relax into simple presence. And that's where it helps to realize how choiceless and impersonal this whole process is. Otherwise we get caught up in self-blame, discouragement, comparing ourselves to others, and stories of being a failure.

But on the other hand, if you lose sight of the response-ability that is Here / Now, you are like a person waiting for grace to open your hand, or like a baby waiting for God to roll you over and move you across the room. You are leaving yourself out of the Totality, separating yourself from God, overlooking the fact that your abilities are part of how God (or Totality) is functioning.

Part of waking up is becoming sensitive to how we become discouraged, how we close down, and where we go for false comfort. To wake up is to become aware of the tendency to judge ourselves, to take our failures personally, to fall into despair, self-pity, depression, frustration, anger, or wherever we tend to go when we believe the story that we are a loser who can't do it right. *Seeing* all of this is enough. Awareness is its own action. We don't need to analyze it mentally or try to impose changes willfully based on our ideas of what "should" be happening, and in fact, that rarely works. Just being awake to the present moment, as it is, and seeing clearly what *is* happening—not what we *think* is happening—this is transformative. The most profound transformation happens when we are not trying to transform, when we are simply awake Here / Now.

Waking up is discerning the difference between the *description* and the *actuality* of this present moment. Liberation is simply *being* the territory itself, that which we already are and cannot *not* be. Confusion is always in the map. Any *story* of improvement (or failure), however relatively true it may appear to be, is one more mirage to see through as it arises. It takes thought, memory and imagination to conjure it up. Wherever you go, Here you are, and there is never any more *here-ness* than there is right now, *whatever* form Here / Now takes.

At the moment of death and every night in deep sleep and actually instant by instant, everything disappears. *We* disappear. In deep sleep, even the first, bare *sense* of awareness or presence disappears. Nothing perceivable or conceivable remains. What a relief! The peace and freedom of deep sleep is a wonderful pointer to falling awake. Falling awake is not some act of rigorous exertion striving for perfection, but rather, it is an absence of concern. It isn't a state of well-maintained, non-stop mindfulness, but rather, a relaxing into the luminous clarity and wakefulness that is never not here.

Here / Now is all there is. Each momentary form, each wave of the ocean, each character in the play of life is a totally unique expression of the whole. In the absolute sense, there are no mistakes. Any apparent dysfunction is all part of the larger functioning. But that doesn't mean we don't fix a flat tire or correct a spelling error. It doesn't mean we can't meditate, see through delusion, cultivate awareness, plan for the future or work to protect the environment. Like the white blood cells cleaning the blood, it's *all* part of the dance. And like a dance, it's all a form of play. It isn't going anywhere. It has no larger purpose.

There is a story about Shankara, the great master of Advaita Vedanta in India. Some of Shankara's students apparently charged him with an elephant to test their teacher's assertion that "It's all One" (or that "It's all a dream"). When Shankara jumped out of the way of the approaching elephant, his students reportedly said, "Ah-ha... you don't really believe that everything is One (or that it's all a dream), because if you did, then why would you jump out of the way?" Whereupon Shankara explained that the One (or the dream) he was talking about included his impulse to jump out of the path of a charging elephant. Likewise, nondual boundlessness includes the aspiration to relieve suffering and it includes the actions that follow from that aspiration. It simply recognizes that *none* of this is "my" doing and that none of it has any inherent, objective reality. Nondual boundlessness also includes acts of destruction and cruelty, again with the recognition that there is no actor behind such actions and that none of it has any enduring reality. Life includes both the cancer cells and the white blood cells, both the predator and the prey, both the parasite and the host, both Hitler and Buddha, and ultimately it's all a dream-like appearance vanishing into thin air.

What should you do? What *are* you doing? *Whatever* you are doing right now is the only possible happening at this moment. In the time it took to read that sentence, everything in the whole universe has completely changed. How real was any of it? You are untouched by anything that happens, not because you are removed or detached, but because you are inseparable. "You" and "the world" are empty of substance, empty of independent existence.

All our suffering and confusion about what to do, all our guilt and blame and shame, all our apparent dilemmas are in the map, not in the territory itself. That's not something to take on faith or to believe. It's something to discover. And this discovery is the activity of the whole universe. It is happening by itself. And like everything, it only happens now.

Control and Surrender

Realizing our true self is letting go. *That's really all it is—just letting go into this openness.... We don't really know how letting go happens. We want to know so we can* make *it happen.... But gradually we find that letting go really isn't our job. Rather, our task is to learn how to let things be exactly as they are.*

—Jon Bernie

Why do you make an effort? Only because you're looking for some result, for something outside yourself.... So first, see how you are constantly making an effort.

—Jean Klein

Discipline is not so much a matter of doing this or that, but of holding still. Not as if this would cost no effort. But the effort is all applied to the crucial task, the task of making no effort.

—Brother David Steindl-Rast, O.S.B.

Effort is a sign of conflict between incompatible desires. They should be seen as they are—then only they dissolve.

—Nisargadatta

The basic nature of our human suffering is very much like an addiction. It is an unskillful, habitual movement away from Here / Now toward something that we imagine will be less painful and more pleasant or exciting, a movement that brings temporary satisfaction followed by ever-increasing dissatisfaction.

Although addictive behavior is by definition out of control, it is paradoxically all about trying to control our experience and make it better than it presently seems to be. And in the short-run, this effort often seems to work. For a moment, we may indeed feel better. But in the long-run, addictive behavior only makes the problem worse. The more we scratch the itch, the more it itches, and pretty soon we have a festering sore.

As we begin to recognize how painful an addiction is, we then start trying to control it. We go to war with it. We try to stop, and when we fail, we feel so terrible about ourselves for having failed that we want to indulge in the addictive activity more than ever so that we can feel better again! We seem to be trapped in a terrible cycle of conflict between opposing desires: the desire to stop and the desire to indulge.

Both of these desires are a movement away from the present actuality of Here / Now and toward something that is imagined to be more desirable. When we want to indulge, we crave the pleasure of the addictive activity, and when we want to stop, we long for the dream of being free from the addiction. *Longing* to stop, thinking we *"should"* stop, *trying* to stop, and this whole conflict between the desire to stop and the desire to indulge—*all* of this is part of the addiction (and is different from actually stopping).

Actually stopping can only happen Here / Now,

and it is not a turning away. It is an opening up that is often described as surrender. Surrender is the end of resistance and seeking (not forever after, but right now). Surrendering is an absolute acceptance of *what is*—not doing anything to move away from *what is* or toward something better. Simply being present at the still point of Here / Now, completely open to life as it is in this moment. Awareness is totally inseparable from everything it touches and reveals. So this is not a detached witnessing that stands back from life, but rather, a total intimacy with life, a total intimacy with this moment, just as it is.

You are no longer judging yourself for being exactly the way you are, or for doing exactly what you are doing in this moment. When resistance and seeking fall away, when judgment and analysis are quiet, what remains?

You may discover that when there is no resistance to totally being in hell, heaven opens up and samsara reveals its true nature as nirvana. But the catch is, if you are embracing hell as a *strategy* to get you to heaven, that doesn't work. Only the complete absence of wanting *what is* to be different in any way pops the imaginary bubble of separation. No one can do this. It is like dying or falling asleep. It is the absence of any doing, the absence of control, the absence of effort, the absence of any concern about what happens. It is a letting go, a dissolving, a relaxing. This letting go begins with letting go even of the need to let go, for the *need* to fall asleep keeps us awake, just as the *imperative* to surrender is a form of holding on and seeking control. True surrender is the absence of resistance even to holding on if that is how life is showing up in this moment. Surrender is the absence of trying to surrender.

With my fingerbiting compulsion, when there is no longer the story of being "me," the one with a terrible, shameful, neurotic problem that "I" need to manage and control and fix so that "I" can finally be okay—when that story ends and there are simply the bare sensations of teeth on fingers and tension in the jaw, it is clear that these sensations and these chewed fingers are no less holy, no less the Masterpiece, than gnarled trees and gale force winds and all the compulsive forces of nature. There is no "Joan" anymore separate from these sensations, no story about what is "enlightened" or "neurotic," no concern with changing any of it, no story about "me" not being as good as Ramana Maharshi. There is simply the inconceivable happening of life, without any separate observer judging or evaluating it. It doesn't matter if Joan has more cloudy weather than somebody else. Joan is fine *exactly* the way she is, and in fact, she is no particular way at all, for everything is always changing. There is no repetition. Every instant is a new universe. Only in thought does it seem to be "the same old me with my same old neurotic habit."

In one sense, this letting go of self-concern happens by grace, and in another sense, as we've talked about, there is a learning that happens (when it does, when the right conditions come together to make it possible), a learning that involves making no effort, doing nothing, simply being just as you are. And this letting go begins and ends with the realization that nothing needs to happen, that *everything* is grace, *just as it is*. It is the *absence* of thinking or believing that something different has to happen.

So if we find ourselves judging and berating ourselves for being caught up in some compulsion, this judging and berating is itself part of the compulsion. To look upon this compulsion as an enemy and then try to fight against or eliminate it by force only strengthens the compulsion and the sense of being a separate somebody who has this compulsion. What actually works is more akin to the martial art Aikido, where they go *with* the energy of the opponent, rather than meeting the opponent head on and trying to over-power them with oppositional brute force. Instead of trying to control things or accomplish something, the focus is simply on being awake Here / Now, and recognizing that this compulsion is another perfect stroke in the Masterpiece.

Being Here / Now does not take time. Whatever takes time is illusory. This is a big clue. Improvement or progress or turning into a "better person" takes time. Seeking takes time. Trying takes time. Getting rid of something takes time. Going on another meditation retreat takes time. "Being in the now" a split second from now takes time. Surrender is timeless and effortless.

Surrender recognizes that *nothing* is outside unicity. The Masterpiece is all there is, and all there is, is the Masterpiece. Even seeking and trying are part of this Masterpiece. There is a natural (compulsory) movement in life to find a way out of suffering. In a certain practical context, this is functional and serves us well. And in nature, not every effort is successful. But if we observe carefully, we may begin to discover that a large part of our human suffering is the *need* and the *effort* to get away from the suffering, and we may find, to our surprise, that the biggest relief is in not needing any relief.

Of course that doesn't mean not taking an aspirin, not going to the dentist, not getting into a recovery program, not going on a meditation retreat, or not fixing a flat tire. It points to something much more immediate.

True freedom is not the liberty to do as we please, but rather, it is the freedom to be as we are. True freedom has no problem with limitation—it is totally free and unlimited within limitation. Freedom is the relaxation that is so relaxed that it has no problem with contracting and tensing up. Life includes contraction *and* expansion, suffering *and* liberation.

Taking liberation and suffering personally, thinking we can have one without the other, is delusion. Liberation *seems* elusive only because it is so all-inclusive, so always already fully present. We overlook it by searching for it. In searching for it, we imagine that we are separate from it, that this isn't it, that "it" is something we can find "out there" somewhere.

No one can choose to begin or end this kind of seeking. It is an impersonal, compulsory happening of life itself. Seeking is only a problem from the perspective of the imaginary seeker who takes the seeking personally and then imagines (and seeks) an end to seeking. But from the perspective of totality, there is no end to seeking. Life, by its very nature, is always seeking something. The river seeks the sea, metal filings seek the magnet, the bee seeks the flower, the flower seeks the sunlight. Certain *forms* of seeking may fall away. Joan is no longer seeking oblivion in alcohol and drugs, for example, nor is she seeking enlightenment anymore. Those particular forms have fallen away. But there is no end to seeking in the larger sense, and no form of seeking *needs* to fall away or be any different in this moment than exactly how it is. There is no seeker (and no finder), and there never has been. There is simply the undivided movement of life.

The best way to end suffering is to completely accept it. And if it persists, be curious about it—watch it closely and see how it unfolds—see what sets it in motion, what keeps it going—see what constitutes it, what it is made of (the thoughts, the sensations, the stories, the activities)—see if all of this is real, if there is anyone doing it—and find out, in this moment right now, if suffering is optional. There is no right or wrong answer. This is a question to live with and to explore.

The Flow: Inhaling and Exhaling

There are two movements or pulls that we can all observe in our lives. One is the movement that seeks to survive as form and that craves experience, and the other is the movement that longs to let go into formlessness and into the absence of experience. One moment we want to run around, do things, make things, tell stories, explore the world. The next moment we want to lie down, close our eyes, let everything fall away and go to sleep. Every day we experience a movement from the formlessness of deep sleep to the forms of dreaming and waking life and then back again to the formlessness of deep sleep. In the course of a year, we experience this same cycle in the seasons, budding and blossoming, coming to fruition and then dying. As a young child, we are hungry to explore the world, to touch everything. In old age, as we move toward death, we are more and more content to do nothing, to sleep, to vanish completely. Life flows naturally through these cycles of darkness and light, summer and winter, birth and death, grasping and relaxing, expanding and contracting, inhaling and exhaling, pleasant experiences and unpleasant experiences. The tide goes in and out, the moon waxes and wanes, all of it one undivided movement.

But we divide it up mentally and take sides. We *think* of ourselves as separate. We think that we are outside the flow of life, or maybe rushing along *in* the flow like a boat going down the rapids. It seems like an urgent necessity that we survive as this apparent form. We think that we have to manage our lives, control the universe, *do* something, make something of ourselves. If we're spiritually inclined, we imagine that we have to somehow *become* the flow or *embody* the flow. Since we already *are* the flow, this effort is really quite comical, like the proverbial fish swimming around in search of water. But we don't see the joke.

It seems as if "I" am the center of the universe and that "my" effort to get somewhere, to become somebody, to survive as this form, and to do it "right", is all very serious and important business. But at the same time, we see that everything dies. Our bodies can be wiped out or totally disabled in an instant. Our houses and cities are routinely blown away by hurricanes, crushed by earthquakes, burned up in fires, blown to bits in wars. We have discovered that our planet is a tiny and vulnerable speck of dust in a vast cosmos. From this vantage point, our life seems utterly insignificant and absurdly meaningless.

There is something in us that knows that everything is okay, that even if the whole universe explodes, all is well. Something in us knows intuitively that everything we can perceive is a kind of dream, and that we are the Ultimate Dreamer, the emptiness that is at once the fabric of every dream and what remains when the dream is gone.

But we forget. We take the dream very seriously. We divide things up and then think that it is either/or, that we must somehow choose between inhaling and exhaling or between the relative and the absolute. We get the idea that what we want is perpetual springtime. We think meditation is spiritual and watching television is a distraction, a "waste of time," a fall from grace, something we "should" avoid. We want to be "in the zone" 24/7. Clinging to the idea of a particular form that has never really existed in the first place, we resist growing old and dying as if these were problems to be vanquished, as if our goal were to keep this form called "me" perpetually young and alive forever. We consume anti-aging potions and have plastic surgery to make ourselves look young again. This is our human suffering, and the joke is, it's all imaginary.

In reality, we're not separate from the flow, nor are we *in* the flow. We *are* the flow. There is *only* flow. We can't *not* be here now.

Every apparent form (including this planet) dies, and along the way, gets bruised, bumped, mangled, broken and incapacitated to one degree or another. But this only seems like a problem when we mistake these apparent forms for separate, independent, persisting entities, rather than recognizing them as momentary appearances in what is actually thorough-going flux.

Whether we are moved to care for an infant, tend a garden, heal an injury, fix what is broken, or whether we are moved to commit murder, get drunk, start a war, or stay in bed all day weeping, *all* of this, including our interest in waking up and our desire to go to sleep, *is* the movement of life. And from the perspective of wholeness, it's not about "up" triumphing permanently over "down," or some imaginary fragment becoming a winner. That's all part of the dream.

Life itself is very simple. The present moment is very simple. But when we try to conceptualize or formulate it, then it *seems* contradictory to the thinking mind. We hear that there is no path, that we're always Here / Now, that "this is it," and yet, there seems to be a kind of progressive journey or shift from confusion and suffering to clarity and liberation. We say it's all unicity, and yet, we can discern a palpable difference between the enlightened sage and the deluded madman, between moments of wakefulness and moments of confusion, between Helen Keller *before* she grokked the word water and Helen Keller *after* that moment in which the whole world of human communication and relationship suddenly opened up to her. We say there is nothing to do, that everything is perfect as it is, but then why are we even bothering to say it?

When we wake up, we get nothing and we've gone nowhere! And yet, waking up is the difference between heaven and hell. But paradoxically, waking up is the realization that the boundless absolute includes *both* heaven *and* hell. The longing to avoid hell and experience only heaven turns out to be an aspect of hell, a kind of entrancement or siren-song. There is no such thing as up without down or a perpetually sunny day. Liberation includes the whole ride, not just the parts we like. Only when we imagine that we are a separate fragment in a fragmented world do we want only heaven and no hell. Liberation is the end of taking it all personally and of trying to have perpetual heaven. Waking up is the willingness to be in hell, the willingness to fail, to have all our human imperfections, to be exactly as we are in this moment.

That doesn't mean we lose all interest in waking up from suffering and delusion, but we know where freedom resides. We know that it's not "out there" somewhere. It's not the result of getting rid of something, or attaining something, or fixing something. It's not some special experience other than the one we're having right now. We understand that the way out of our suffering is in no longer needing a way out!

What If We Really Are Perfect, Just As We are?

You can't not be in grace. Everything about you is totally absolutely perfectly appropriate. All the things you think are wrong with you are absolutely right.

—Tony Parsons

No creature ever comes short of its own completeness. Wherever it stands, it does not fail to cover the ground.

—Dogen

Not in your drunkest, sorriest, most hysterical moments, not even then can you fall out of this clear and sacred perfection.

—J. Matthews

We want to be only good, and we want to remove all evil. But that is because we forget that good is made of non-good elements.... You cannot be good alone. You cannot hope to remove evil, because thanks to evil, good exists, and vice versa.

—Thich Nhat Hanh

May it be as it is.

—Karl Renz

My karate teacher used to say that the mark of a true master was not perfection, but rather, the ability to keep going when you made a mistake as if nothing had happened—to keep going as if the mistake you made were absolutely perfect.

In contrast to this, our habitual tendency when we make a mistake is often to collapse in humiliation and despair and give up. We get easily lost in regret, disappointment, self-blame and self-hatred. We take our apparent failures personally.

What would it mean to really *get* that we are perfect just as we are?

When we realize that *everything* that appears to happen is an expression of the One Reality, then we realize there is really no way to fail. We are the whole world—we are Buddha and Hitler, wisdom and foolishness, good and evil, clarity and confusion—the whole package. We are no longer obsessed with making "me" a success, being Number One, winning the game or becoming perfect. We may still want to do our best, but not so we can get someplace better and out-shine everyone else and "be somebody" at last.

I've heard that in Tibetan Buddhism, there is a prayer that says: "Help me to see the futility of everything." I don't hear this as a statement of nihilistic despair, but rather as a recognition that nothing is going anywhere, for it is already here, fully complete. Whatever happens, it's all part of the show, and the beauty of the show is that it has no meaning beyond itself. Instead of "May it be as I'd like it to be," our prayer becomes, "May it be as it is."

When we look closely, we find that we can't actually separate the light from the dark. For example, being a drunk and a heavy drug user in my late teens and early twenties may have damaged my brain and my health in various ways, and as a drunk, I did many destructive things that were hurtful to myself and others. But I also gained a certain wisdom, insight and compassion that I might not have gained in any other way. So was my alcohol and drug abuse ultimately a "bad" thing? And what about my fingerbiting compulsion, which has taught me so much about the compulsory nature of life and the peace that comes with acceptance—would my life or the universe as a whole have been better had I been spared this compulsion? Can we say that it would have been "better" for the universe if the holocaust had never happened, or if Thich Nhat Hanh had not had to live through the horrors of the Vietnam War, or if Shunryu Suzuki and Ramana Maharshi and Nisargadatta Maharaj had not all died of cancer, or if Alan Watts and Chogyam Trungpa had not both had as much to drink as they each did, or if Osho had not had his ninety-six Rolls-Royces? Everything *is* as it is. And as Thich Nhat Hanh points out, roses and garbage are inseparable—the rose depends on the compost, and the compost depends on the rose—they contain each other as one undivided process that he calls *interbeing*. And in the final analysis, our whole life and this whole universe is like a snowflake hitting the warm ground. Poof! It's gone! How real was it?

A friend recently wrote to me that he was seeing the image of Jesus on the cross in a wholly new way, as a pointer to the sacredness of *everything*. "It is *God* hanging on the cross," he wrote, "spikes through hands and feet, showing that even this suffering is sacred, is God, is Emptiness, is Just This."

Perfection is not someplace else that we hope to someday arrive at—a magical place where our neurosis is totally gone, our arthritis healed, our partner behaving exactly as we want, our noisy neighbors finally silent, and the world transformed at last into a peaceful and loving utopia. This is a fantasy. It is one half of a pair. Perfection is the whole enchilada. It includes everything. Even God nailed to a cross.

The Pathless Path to Here / Now

Your true nature is something never lost to you even in moments of delusion, nor is it gained at the moment of Enlightenment.... I assure you that all things have been free from bondage since the very beginning.

—Huang Po

You can't put a foot wrong, because nothing and no one is going anywhere. "You" are not a character on a journey to self-realisation. It's all a play of appearances.

—Nathan Gill

The infinite is not somewhere else waiting for us to become worthy.

—Tony Parsons

As you walk the spiritual path, it widens, not narrows, until one day it broadens to a point where there is no path left at all.

—Wayne Liquorman

The pathless path from here to here is an imaginary journey, somewhat like Dorothy's journey from Kansas to Oz and back. Like Dorothy, we end up right where we started. In reality, we've gone nowhere, for Now / Here is all there is. But the stories and beliefs that confuse us into thinking otherwise have become transparent, allowing the ever-present obvious to emerge into full awareness.

When we think back, there *appears* to have been a journey over time or maybe a sudden moment of awakening sometime in the past, but all of this is a kind of dream. It takes memory and imagination to conjure it up. We haven't really gone anywhere. We've always been right here. It's always been now. And in fact, "we" are only a mirage.

Often we have the idea that the spiritual path involves working very hard to cleanse and purify ourselves. We think our goal is to get rid of anger, depression, confusion, anxiety, addiction, laziness and everything we consider "negative" and "unenlightened." We think that we must strive to become someone who always feels awake, happy, zestful and expanded, someone who exudes loving-kindness and who never gets upset or defensive. We're trying to turn "The Bad Me" into "A Good Me," which works about as well as trying to turn Chicago into Los Angeles. We imagine spiritual practice to be a kind of policing operation in which we endeavor to control, improve, polish and perfect ourselves until finally we achieve our Ideal Self, the Enlightened Me who is perfectly me-less at last. We want to become *somebody* who has no self and no flaws. But this whole endeavor is a total misunderstanding of the pathless path. This approach leads to momentary highs (often accompanied by uptightness, self-righteousness or grandiosity) followed by frustration, disappointment, discouragement and the story of being a failure.

Trying to be in any particular experiential state "all the time" is suffering. It doesn't work. Instead of focusing primarily on the *differences* between one experience and another, we may begin to notice what is the same in every different experience, whether it is a contracted experience or an expanded experience, whether there is thinking or no thinking, whether we are washing the dishes mindfully or doing them on autopilot, whether we are making love with our partner or yelling at them, whether we are watching a crime drama on TV or sitting in meditation—the beingness, the *here-ness,* the *now-ness,* the *suchness* is ever-present, like the water in every wave.

Sometimes what we think of as enlightenment shows up Here / Now, and sometimes what we think of as delusion shows up, and we begin to realize that there is no "owner" of either one of these appearances. They are impersonal, interdependent aspects of one, undivided whole. Boundless unicity includes *both* enlightenment *and* delusion.

Enlightenment recognizes that *everything* is the Holy Reality, even delusion! Whereas delusion seeks the Holy Reality "out there" and imagines that "this isn't it." Delusion takes everything that happens personally, whereas enlightenment sees that nothing is personal. Enlightenment loves everything unconditionally and sees only God everywhere, while delusion sees enemies and obstructions, things that need to be vanquished and eliminated.

Planning a genocide comes from delusion. It requires extreme dualistic thinking. But in seeing only God everywhere, even the genocide is recognized as the Holy Reality in thin disguise. There is *nothing* that is not unicity. Enlightenment recognizes that there is no enlightenment without delusion, that enlightenment and delusion arise together, while delusion is at war with delusion. Delusion wants to cleanse the universe of delusion.

Enlightenment recognizes unicity but doesn't deny the difference between apples and oranges. Enlightenment doesn't mix up relative and absolute, whereas delusion is always fixating and getting stuck on one side or the other of an imaginary divide.

Every night in deep sleep, everything perceivable and conceivable vanishes completely, and the one who cares about getting enlightened vanishes as well. This is peace. Enlightenment recognizes that this absolute peace is ever-present, that it is the very *nature* of Here / Now. The absence that is present in deep sleep (the absence of both presence and absence, the absence of concern, the absence of separation) is what Here / Now *is*. *All* experiences, the whole movie of waking life, all the delusion and all the clarity, even the most sublime awakening experiences, even enlightenment itself, are all dreamlike appearances. None of it really matters in the way we imagined it did. Everything perceivable and conceivable is *in* the movie, even the first, barest *sense* of aware presence. Our True Nature, the Ultimate Subject, the groundless ground, is inconceivable.

And yet, this absolute absence is not *other* than the sound of traffic and the taste of tea right here, right now. Form is emptiness and emptiness is form. These are merely different words for one seamless reality.

The more I tune into the bare actuality of Here / Now, the more there is a falling away of all attempts to define *what is*.

As we walk the pathless path, the dividing line between "meditation" or "satsang" and "the rest of life" gradually dissolves, along with any notion of what is "spiritual" or "not spiritual." We are no longer *trying* very hard to be mindful as we wash the dishes, or *trying* very hard to identify ourselves as awareness and not as the character, or *trying* very hard to observe and "be aware" and not get caught up in our drama. *All* of that spiritual efforting disappears. There may still be a devotion to presence and an interest in seeing through illusion. We may still meditate, go to satsang or read nondual books, but it happens without gaining ideas, without expectations, without any added purpose other than simply doing it because it is the happening of life.

Special experiences may happen, but they are not important. This isn't about having experiences. Nor is it about philosophy. Nonduality is not a philosophy anymore than the taste of coffee or the sound of traffic is philosophy. This is waking up from philosophy.

If thought pops up and says, "I only have an intellectual understanding, not an actual, direct experience," this is a thought and it tells a story. If this story is believed, immediately we begin seeking some special experience other than the one we are actually having right now. But who is it that has this problem? Who is this "me" who supposedly hasn't had a direct experience yet? And where would we find this experience other than Here / Now? Is there not an undeniable direct experiencing right now (hearing, seeing, sensing, awaring, breathing, being)? Be aware of how thought pops up and creates the imaginary problem and then tries to solve it. This isn't about having some special experience that you've never had or that you remember having once years ago, but rather, it's about noticing the actual *experiencing* that is Here / Now, no matter what form it takes. That takes no effort because it is already the case. It's simply the falling away of the *idea* that "this isn't it."

Does liberation or enlightenment or awakening take effort and practice? Maybe, maybe not. It takes what it takes to realize that nothing is needed to be what you already are. The trick is that this realization is not a *belief* that we can arrive at intellectually and then super-impose upon life, but rather, it is a present moment *seeing through* of the thoughts that create the illusory problem—thoughts like "I'm not there yet," or "This isn't it," or "If only I could stop getting caught up in all these false thoughts, then I'd be enlightened." Seeing the false as false is the spontaneous activity of Life Itself.

There is no one-size-fits-all spiritual practice or pointer. One person will gravitate to a highly structured approach, another to an approach that is more open and spontaneous. For some, meditating daily on a schedule or practicing with a group may be essential. For others, these activities just get in the way. What we need in one moment may be different from what we need in another moment. There is no one right way. This universe is magnificently diverse and playful. And of course, any person or activity that we later identify as "the cause of our awakening" is just one link in an infinite chain of dream-like events, a network that includes everything in the whole universe. Our worst mistakes are as essential to this imaginary process as our greatest insights. True awakening is simply the realization that no one was ever bound in the first place. Ultimate Reality is uncaused and unconditioned. Nothing brings it about, for it is all there is. It has never been absent. We never really need to be worrying about what we "should" do. We can rest assured that we are always already doing it, that it is exactly what is presently arising, just as it is.

And if we can't stop worrying, no problem. This, too, is only a movement of energy, a fleeting appearance in a dream. This whole movie of waking life, our entire spiritual adventure, *anything* we can experience, all the worries and all the moments of bliss, everything perceivable and conceivable, all of it is no more substantial than a dream. Trying to get out of the dream is part of the dream. The one who wants to escape the dream is a character in the dream. The Ultimate Dreamer is already outside the dream, unbound by the dream, and the dream itself is only an appearance. All the forms that appear in this dream-like movie of waking life (buildings, cars, people, thoughts, feelings, emotions) are as impermanent and as insubstantial as cloud formations. Whatever seemingly important changes occur in the movie of waking life are like the changes that occur in a dream. They *seem* to matter greatly during the dream, *in the context of the dream,* but in waking up, the whole world of the dream disappears completely. Waking up is the end of spirituality in the usual sense of that word.

With that in mind, we can approach various nondual explorations (or practices, if you want to call them that) in a playful way, as natural and spontaneous activities of life. Like art, music or dancing, they are ways in which life is exploring, enjoying, revealing, loving and entertaining itself. It is all an infinite, never-ending Self-realization.

The Art of Going Nowhere

Meditating is like inviting fire into our consciousness....In the realm of true meditation there is no such thing as a meditator or meditation. There is nothing to be done.

—Anam Thubten

One relaxes into an uncontrived, open spaciousness which is neither a state of self-conscious meditation nor an inattentive state of distraction.

—Steven Batchelor

Stay without ambition, without the least desire, exposed, vulnerable, unprotected, uncertain and alone, completely open to and welcoming life as it happens, without the selfish conviction that all must yield you pleasure or profit, material or so-called spiritual.

—Nisargadatta Maharaj

Practice is not about having nice feelings, happy feelings. It's not about changing, or getting somewhere. That in itself is the basic fallacy. But observing this desire begins to clarify it. We begin to comprehend that our frantic desire to get better, to "get somewhere," is illusion itself, and the source of suffering.

—Charlotte Joko Beck

Meditation begins now, *right* here. *It can't
begin someplace else or at some other time.… In
meditation we return to where we already are—this
shifting, changing ever-present* now.

—Steve Hagen

The word "meditation" gets used to mean so many different things, and people take up meditation for so many
different reasons, that I tend to avoid the word altogether.
What I invite people to explore is simply being awake
Here / Now, being aware, giving open attention to actual
direct experience, without looking upon anything that
happens as a distraction or an interruption, without trying to change or modify it in any way.

This can happen while sitting quietly in an armchair,
or it can happen on the city bus while riding to work, or
it can happen in a waiting room before a medical appointment, or on an airplane, or on a bench in the park. It can
happen while walking through nature or while walking
through the city. It can happen in your kitchen or in
a prison cell, in a hospital bed or at the office. For one
moment (whether that moment lasts for a few seconds, a
few minutes, a few hours, or a few days), as an experi-
ment, put down the magazines, the books, the iPod, the
smart phone. Turn off the computer, the radio, the TV.
Put down your knitting and your prayer beads. And
simply be present, empty-handed. See what reveals itself.

The whooshing of traffic, the song of a bird, the
faint sound of a television in another room. Rain drops
hanging on a green leaf, a cigarette butt in the gutter,
clouds drifting across the blue sky. The fragrance of

flowers, the smell of exhaust fumes from the city bus, the sweetness of rain-drenched air. Breathing, tightness in the chest, queasiness in the belly, an ache in the shoulder, a sensation of heat or cold. The spaciousness that permeates it all.

This kind of exploration brings you out of the mental realm of thoughts and into the nonconceptual realm of sensory awareness. It gives you a direct, felt-experience of fluidity, impermanence and spaciousness. Breath, sounds and sensations cannot be grasped or held onto—they are a movement without borders or seams. Actually, thinking and conceptualizing are also a movement without borders or seams, but it's much easier to notice that with sense perceptions than it is with thoughts and ideas. So by simply being here as thoughtless awareness, you experience directly that everything is changing and that all of life is seamless, undivided movement or presence. There is no distance between you and this present happening. It is utterly immediate. You *are* this.

As thoughts pop up, is it possible to see that they are only thoughts, that perhaps they don't need to be followed or believed, that they are not the objective reports on reality they claim to be? Can you see how these thoughts instantly create mental movies and stories, and how seductive these stories are, how real they seem? Can you notice the difference between thinking and sensing?

By simply giving attention to the present moment, you may discover how suffering is created and sustained and whether there is a way of meeting pain or painful circumstances without suffering. You may wake up to the exquisite beauty and perfection of everything, just as it is. This is true meditation, but we don't need to call it meditation, and it is probably best not to call it anything.

This simple awakeness may happen in a formal way or it may happen spontaneously in your kitchen while drinking a cup of coffee. However it happens is the only possible way that it *can* happen in this moment. If Zen practice shows up in your movie of waking life, then for you, Zen practice is apparently necessary, until (perhaps) it isn't. For another, the same insights that come to you through Zen practice might come while sitting on a park bench or raising a child. There is no one right path, and ultimately, there is no path at all. There is only Here / Now.

In my story, I went from formal Zen practice to being with Toni Packer, a former Zen teacher who left the tradition, hierarchy, rituals, ceremonies and dogmas of Zen behind. I lived and worked at Toni Packer's retreat center for five years. We still had silent retreats where we sat in meditation for long periods of time, but the schedule was always optional, we could sit in armchairs and recliners as well as on meditation cushions, we could walk through the woods or take a nap whenever we felt like it, and there was no "practice" in the usual sense—no counting the breath or working on a koan—we were simply invited to be aware of whatever was actually happening, to feel the breathing and hear the sounds of the rain, and to investigate the sense of a separate "me" and see if it was real. From there, I got involved in the Advaita satsang world, and finally with radical nonduality. Formal meditation fell away for the most part, although I continue to enjoy being silent and "doing nothing" whenever it invites me, but I no longer think of it as "meditation."

When I invite any kind of meditative exploration now, I'm not suggesting a deliberate "practice" in the sense of sitting in some special upright posture counting the breath, repeating a mantra, or *trying* very hard to "be present." I'm not *against* any of that if you're drawn to it, but what I'm pointing to is something much more simple. I'm pointing to a way of being that is open and effortless. That doesn't mean that you just sink mindlessly into non-stop daydreams or wallow in obsessive thoughts and stories, although that will happen from time to time, but perhaps when it does, and when you notice it, you might see if it is possible to let go and fall back into the effortless simplicity of nonconceptual experiencing: hearing the traffic, feeling the breathing, listening to the rain, sensing the body, feeling heat or cold – simply being awake to the bare actuality of whatever is showing up, however it is.

Your whole life involves all kinds of activities and states of mind, so I'm not suggesting that you should try to do this kind of meditative exploration "all the time." On the other hand, what I'm pointing to isn't something *apart* from the rest of your life that you just do once a day while sitting on a cushion in the lotus position. It is your whole life. But that doesn't mean never watching television or trying to be continuously aware of all your thoughts, sensations and behaviors.

This kind of exploration is not intended as a goal-oriented, self-improvement task. At best, it may reveal something about the nature of reality by occasionally slowing things down a bit, simplifying the situation and stripping away many of the things that typically captivate our attention, thus allowing what is often overlooked to come to light. But don't imagine that *something* in particular will come to light. This is not about having some special experience or getting some special understanding. It's nothing more or less than the utter simplicity of what is, just as it is.

If you *do* notice yourself following any of these suggestions in an effortful way with the idea of improving or getting somewhere, simply notice this movement of the mind, see it for what it is, notice the tension in it, and if you can, relax back into the simplicity of the present moment (hearing, seeing, sensing, awaring, being). And if you can't relax, then simply allow yourself to be tense. Tension is nothing more than an energetic movement – there's nothing wrong with it. It's not "bad." It might be painful, but life includes pain. Liberation is the freedom for life to be exactly *as it is*, not as it *might* be, *could* be or *should* be. You're not going anywhere. Here / Now is all there is, and it's already fully present.

When you stop all your usual activities and rest as open awareness, you may find that thinking runs wild. Instead of feeling blissful and calm, it may *seem* that you are thinking more than ever before. More likely, you are simply more *aware* of compulsive thinking than ever before, and of course, *trying* not to think is a losing battle. So if this happens, simply be *aware* of thinking, and whenever possible, relax back into simple presence – hearing the sounds of traffic or bird songs, experiencing the sensations in the body, feeling the breathing, noticing the spacious openness of this boundless presence that includes everything and resists nothing.

When people first sit down in meditation or go on a silent retreat, with all their usual activities stripped away and nothing to do but *be*, it is not uncommon to go through a kind of withdrawal. Disturbing feelings and sensations can show up, including that basic root sense of discontent, restlessness and unease that motivates so much of our human activity. But if you simply sit with the bare sensations of this discomfort and allow it all to be just as it is, you may find that it is quite bearable and maybe even interesting. A natural curiosity may develop, an interest in exploring this basic unease, finding out what it is, not by thinking about it, labeling it or telling a story about it, but by going all the way to the bottom of it with awareness. You may discover that this unease doesn't stay the same and that at the core of it there is *nothing* at all.

It's also not uncommon for people who take up meditation to begin noticing all kinds of things about themselves they hadn't seen before. If you notice yourself (or other people) behaving in ways that don't fit with your ideas of how you (or others) should be—if you see yourself (or someone else) being manipulative, vengeful, passive-aggressive, self-pitying, self-absorbed, stingy, judgmental, self-righteous, pushy, fawning or whatever it might be, perhaps you will also be able to see that no one is in control of any of this. You are not deliberately choosing to be the way you are in this moment and neither is anyone else. Everything happens by itself. You may begin to see that your thoughts are like secretions of the brain that emerge unbidden, and that your impulses, urges and actions come out of life itself. And you may begin to notice that there is a bigger context, that you are the boundless awareness in which your character appears, that you are being and beholding the whole show. You may find that there is room in this vastness for all the apparent defects and imperfections of life to be exactly as they are.

When we realize that we contain the whole universe, that we have the seeds of both Buddha and Hitler within us, that we *are* the whole show, then we begin to have a natural compassion for everyone and everything being exactly the way it is. We don't take the whole mess so seriously anymore.

So this isn't about eliminating your defects and experiencing only bliss and calm. It is about being awake to life just as it is. And if suffering arises—if you find yourself seemingly trapped in painful, compulsive behavior, if you are feeling depressed, anxious, angry or sad, if you are in physical pain or discomfort, if you are in an environment or a situation that you consider unpleasant or undesirable—you might see if it is possible to simply experience whatever unpleasant or unsettling sensations are showing up without trying to make any of it go away, without seeking a result from this exploration, without trying to understand the situation or analyze it or fix it, without judging it—but simply *experiencing* it *just as it is.*

You might notice how thought wants to move away from the simplicity of this bare experiencing, how it creates the mirage-like sufferer and the idea of time (the endless replaying of past events, the dread of future misery, the hope of a future solution). Our habitual reaction to suffering is to *think* about the apparent problem—go over and over what happened, label it, construct stories about it, analyze it, assign blame, pass judgment, imagine positive and negative future scenarios, search for a fix: *This is unbearable. What if it gets worse? This will kill me. Why is this happening to me? I can't believe you did that to me. This is unfair. I'm such a jerk. I can't do anything right. What if...? If only.... Maybe I should....*

Is it possible to listen to all these thoughts in the same way you might listen to the sounds of wind and rain, as an impersonal happening of nature? Is it possible to let the thoughts go, to shift attention away from the stories and back to the bare actuality of this moment—the sensations in the body, the sounds of traffic, the sense of presence? What happens to the suffering when there is simply the nonconceptual, energetic, naked actuality of this moment? You may discover that the whole story of your life is not as solid as it seems to be and that it takes thought and imagination to keep suffering and misery going.

In simply being present to whatever arises without moving away, we learn that it is possible to be open to these unpleasant or scary experiences that we often think will kill us or not be survivable—pain, uneasiness, anxiety, depression, anger, sadness, fear. By simply being present without moving away, we discover that if we don't scratch an itch, eventually it goes away. Likewise, with pain, we find that by resisting it, by tensing up against it, by trying to escape it, the pain gets worse and seems overwhelming, whereas when we can completely open to it and relax into it, the pain is no longer overwhelming and may even become interesting. We discover, by observing it closely, that "pain" is not a solid thing, but rather, it is made up of ever-changing vibrations that come and go. Of course, sometimes we *do* run away or scratch the itch. It happens. It happens because of infinite causes and conditions and in that moment could not be otherwise. So this isn't about beating ourselves up when reality fails to measure up to our perfectionistic ideals. It is *seeing through* all of that.

In Zen, lots of attention is given to breathing, posture, how you clean the toilet, how you enter and exit the meditation hall, how you hold your rice bowl. To the newcomer who is avidly seeking enlightenment, this focus on the simplest details of ordinary existence seems completely beside the point and absurdly superficial and petty. But in fact, it is a way of pointing the student to *this* moment and undermining the habitual tendency to think *about* reality and get lost in abstractions and ideologies. It is a way of saying that enlightenment is now or never—it's not theoretical, philosophical, metaphysical or mystical—it's utterly simple—it's right here in *this* breath, *this* cup of coffee, *this* toilet bowl. So don't miss it by looking somewhere else. As my first Zen teacher said to me, form is not sacred, but form allows the sacred to emerge.

You begin to notice that *every* experience reveals the ever-present awakeness that is never not here, like the screen that allows every image in the movie to appear and that is visible *as* every scene of the movie regardless of whether it is a scene of violence or a scene of tenderness, or like the mirror that is equally present in and *as* every reflection, or the water that is manifesting as every wave; that awakeness is ever-present *in spite* of what appears, never *because* of what appears. Just as every element in a dream belongs to the dreamer, in the same way, whatever appears in the movie of waking life is never anything *other* than You (the One-without-a-second) surprising yourself with ever-new disguises and ever-new facets of yourself.

When this is seen, you may still have opinions and take appropriate actions in the movie of waking life to do what seems best, but you are no longer acting from a place of false certainty or imaginary separation. You recognize that all the different characters in the play—the good guys and the bad guys—are yourself. Even when it all *seems* very serious, there is a recognition of the bigger context and a knowingness that all of it is a play without substance.

And if you notice yourself rejecting, resisting or judging what shows up, taking it all very seriously, arguing with the way life is, feeling irritated, upset or outraged, this can be a wonderful opportunity to question who or what is feeling threatened and what is at the root of this upset. You may find that at the bottom-line, it is always about the imaginary "me," and it always boils down to a fear of death, a fear of annihilation. Something seems threatening to "me" and my survival. These threats may be *relatively* real in some situations, but in a deeper sense, no-*thing* is ever actually happening in the way we *think* it is. Whatever appears, when investigated closely, is seen to be empty of enduring form or substance. We may discover there is no one to be hurt and nothing that can hurt us. Of course, that doesn't mean walking in front of a bus or not feeling physical or emotional pain anymore. It simply means that nothing sticks.

When people first take up meditation or any other spiritual practice, or when they first go to a meeting or pick up a book about radical nonduality, they usually *imagine* that this is about self-improvement and getting somewhere. The pathless path (the direct path) is actually all about *seeing through* such ideas. Ultimately, it is about seeing that there is no "self" here who is separate from the rest of the universe. There is no "me" who is going back and forth between clarity and confusion, between "getting it" and "losing it," between identification as boundless awareness and identification as the character. The boundary between "spirituality" and "the rest of life" doesn't really exist. There is only the boundless immediacy of Here / Now — just as it is.

All states and experiences come and go. The non-dual absolute is not an experience, nor is it a state that "the person" enters, permanently or temporarily. "The person" is a momentary appearance that comes and goes within nondual boundlessness.

Liberation is loving *what is*—loving yourself, exactly as you are, loving the world, exactly as it is, loving life, warts and all. So play your part, exactly the way you are playing it, which you can't not do, and enjoy the show. You're already Home. You always have been. There is truly no way *not* to be Here / Now. Failure is not even possible.

We are never really in the bondage we imagine ourselves to be trapped in. The problem we are trying so hard to solve is imaginary. The "me" we are trying to improve doesn't even exist. True meditation is discovering all of that directly, not sometime in the future through years of arduous practice, not yesterday in some remembered awakening experience, not once-and-for-all, but right now. The path is always only Here / Now. And the most liberating insight is that *nothing* is needed. This is already it, just as it is.

Inquiry: What is It?

*The penetration of this mystery requires that one
not foreclose it by substituting an answer, be it a
metaphysical proposition or a religious belief. One
has to learn how to suspend the habit of reaching
for a word or phrase with which to fill the emptiness
opened by the question.*

— Steven Batchelor

*When we start inquiring into what is holding
us back from realizing the truth, we come to the
realization that there is really nothing there. There
are no obstacles.*

—Anam Thubten

*Self-inquiry directly leads to Self-realization by
removing the obstacles which make you think that
the Self is not already realized.*

—Ramana Maharshi

*Who (or what) am I?
What is this right here, right now?
When everything perceivable and
conceivable disappears, what remains?
What was your face before your parents were born?*

To whom is all of this happening?

These questions are not asking for conceptual answers. The thinking mind is in the business of finding answers. That's its job. It's a survival function. And in a certain realm, it works beautifully. But when it comes to these ultimate questions, it doesn't work at all. Any answers we come up with are just dead words, dead ideas.

Grasping is one of our earliest and most primal survival reflexes. We grasp with our hands, with our gut, and with our minds. Our human conditioning reinforces the tendency to grasp for answers. In school, we are rewarded for having the right answers, and we feel stupid if we don't know. So, it may be very uncomfortable and unfamiliar at first to not reach for an answer.

The questions posed in nonconceptual, meditative inquiry are of a different nature than the questions posed to us in school. These meditative questions are not looking for answers, although we can easily supply answers with the thinking mind. If we've been around the spiritual scene for any time at all, we probably know all the "correct" answers to these questions. *What am I?* "Pure Consciousness," we might think. Or (if we haven't read very many spiritual books yet), we might say, "me," or give our name. Or (another "advanced" answer) we might say, "Nothing at all." Or, "empty space." Or, "The One Self." If we look at our computer and ask, *What is it?* We might say, "My computer," or we might be more sophisticated and say, "energy," or "consciousness," or "Oneness," or "emptiness." But notice right now that these are all words. Labels. They may be pointing to something that is not a word and not a concept. But the words themselves are not that to which they point.

It's relatively easy to learn the right answers, the right words—to talk the talk. But these questions are inviting something else entirely. They are inviting us to fall into the open space of not knowing, to *"suspend the habit of reaching for a word or phrase with which to fill the emptiness opened by the question."* These questions invite us to discover what can never really be put into words or concepts, although words can certainly be used to describe or point to it.

Inquiry can also mean living with a question that interests us. For example, *Is there free will?* Or, *Who makes choices?* Or, *How does a decision actually happen?*

Instead of looking to see what others have said about this subject and then giving the "correct" answer, whatever we think that might be, inquiry invites us to look and listen and see for ourselves. How *do* we make decisions? This is a wonderful question to explore by carefully and closely observing decision-making as it happens. So as we go about our daily activities, we might begin to actually watch, very closely, as choices happen. It could be little ones like whether to get up after you've been sitting down for awhile, or big ones like whether to get married or take a new job. Really watch closely and carefully as the process unfolds. Notice the back and forth thoughts that pop up by themselves making a case for this direction or that direction. See if you can catch the decisive moment when one side finally wins out and if you can find anyone in control of how that happens. See if you can find the "you" who seems to be authoring your thoughts. Can this thinker or decider at the helm actually be found? Investigate all of this not by thinking about it, but by giving it careful attention with awareness.

Are you in control of the thoughts that arise? Do you know what your next thought will be? Even if you *seem* to be "choosing" to think positive thoughts, from where does the urge and the intention and the ability to do this arise? Does it always work?

You may find that decisions *happen*, and that you cannot pin down exactly how they occur or what sets them in motion. We have stories about "free will" and "determinism," but in the end, these are only conceptual models. Like the pictures in the anatomy book, they can never capture the fluidity and the messiness of life itself.

This kind of meditative inquiry begins with letting all your answers and beliefs go, and not knowing what you'll find, always being open to the possibility of seeing something entirely new and unexpected.

Liberation isn't about finally getting the right answer or picking up a winning solution. It is about *seeing through* the imaginary problem (the misconception) at the root of our suffering and confusion. Any answer, any solution we pick up and stick to is a new problem. Inquiry dissolves all the answers.

Inquiry is also a way of questioning all our thoughts and beliefs. If thought pops up and says, "I've ruined my life," or "He shouldn't have done that," or "The country will be destroyed if she wins the election," no matter how convincing and reasonable these thoughts may seem, we might ask of any such thought: *Can I absolutely know that this is true? How do I feel when this thought is believed? What would it feel like if this thought were not believed?* Don't look for the answers by thinking, but rather, feel into these questions deeply with the whole body and mind. See what reveals itself. You may find that you cannot be completely certain of anything except being here now, and you may find that without your beliefs, you'd be totally happy and okay.

Unlike seeking, which is result-oriented and rooted in a sense of dissatisfaction and incompleteness, this kind of meditative inquiry is rooted in curiosity, interest and love. Much as a lover explores the beloved, this nondual, nonconceptual inquiry is an act of love and devotion. Much as a child explores the world with open curiosity and wonder, this kind of inquiry is a form of play and self-discovery. It is not something you finish doing. Seeking answers and experiences can fall away (if you're lucky). But inquiry is a life-long exploration and discovery that is never finished. It is a way of being. In fact, it is the very nature of life itself.

Turning to Face the Imaginary Tiger

Nondual exploration and meditative inquiry is a hands-on kind of approach. It's not mental or abstract. It's direct and experiential. Rather than trying to paper over our suffering with comforting beliefs, this approach is about actually exploring directly what *seems* to be in the way of freedom, peace and happiness, what *seems* scary, dreadful and unbearable. It's one thing to *believe* that the tiger chasing you is only a mirage, and it's another thing entirely to actually turn around and embrace the tiger and find out for sure.

This embracing is not something you do once and then it's done. It's something that can happen whenever a tiger shows up. Some people have more tigers showing up than others. Comparing yourself to others or wondering when you'll finally be done with your last tiger is delusion. And you can only do what you can do. Sometimes you don't turn and embrace the tiger—sometimes fear overwhelms you, old habits take over, and you run away instead. You flee into whatever it is that offers comfort and escape. And that's okay. Perfectionism is just another imaginary tiger. So if running away happens, if you wake up with a hangover, full of despair, then you start here, where you are, right now. You turn to meet the hangover and the despair. That's your new tiger.

And this "turning and meeting" is not some effortful self-improvement project that you grit your teeth and work really hard at. It's not about being spiritually correct. It's a surrender, a relaxing, an opening up, a letting go, a dissolving. Not doing anything at all.

Here/Now isn't always blissful. It can be anything but blissful. But paradoxically, it is through allowing it all to be as it is in this moment and not moving away that we begin to discover where bliss (or joy, or peace, or love, or freedom) truly resides, and what gets in the way. We begin to realize that the only bliss is right here in the heart of this moment. And that suffering is running away or seeking it elsewhere—"out there" somewhere—in the future, someplace else.

The mind always tends toward fixation and reification. Enlightenment is about waking up from our stories and ideas and beliefs about how it is, our descriptions and labels. It is a pathless path going nowhere (Now / Here). There is nothing to attain, and nothing to fear.

And when it looks otherwise, then simply turn to embrace the tiger, and see for yourself.

Am I Enlightened Yet?

If you wait for an event to take place, for the coming of reality, you will wait forever, for reality neither comes nor goes.

—Nisargadatta Maharaj

Enlightenment is not like a sudden realization of something mysterious. Enlightenment is nothing but awakening from illusions and returning to the reality of life.

—Uchiyama

Awakening in its essence is simply being here.

—Jon Bernie

Enlightenment is not what you think but rather the ultimate, unimaginable dissolution into all that IS.

—Wayne Liquorman

The Self is ever realized, and whoever claims to be realized for sure is a bogus fraud.

—Karl Renz

Spiritual liberation frees you from the misery-inducing fantasy of perfecting yourself.

—Darryl Bailey

Waking up is a continuing process. No one wakes up once and for all. There is no limit to wakefulness, just as there is no limit to aliveness... The surprise within the surprise of every new discovery is that there is ever more to be discovered.

—Brother David Steindl-Rast, O.S.B.

Words such as "awakening" or "enlightenment" or "waking up" or "liberation" are all so potentially misleading that I am always tempted not to use any of these words ever again. Why? Because the only forever is now. Because there is no light apart from the dark, and no enlightenment apart from delusion. Because there is no permanently enlightened person. The very notion of such a thing is delusion. So-called awakening isn't personal. It doesn't happen *to me*. The wave has *never* been anything other than water waving. Once people start identifying themselves or others as "permanently enlightened people," the bullshit begins.

Since everything is changing, what we call "a person" is not really the same from one instant to the next. No continuous form exists, and nothing stands apart from everything else in the universe. So who exactly would be enlightened?

Any so-called "awakened or enlightened person," if we can speak of such a thing at all, is only enlightened Here / Now, not forever after, because there *is* no forever after. There is *only* Here / Now. So-called awakening or enlightenment is the realization that this boundlessness is not encapsulated inside a person, that there is only seamless unicity from which nothing stands apart.

One contemporary Zen teacher compares an enlightened being to a pedestrian as a way of illustrating the momentary and ungraspable nature of any such apparent being. When the pedestrian sits down, what happens to the pedestrian? There isn't one! It's like asking what happens to my fist when I open my hand, or what happens to my lap when I stand up. The awakened being (like the pedestrian, the fist or the lap) is an *activity*, a momentary forming of the undivided formlessness.

Of course, *relatively* speaking, for practical purposes, we can say that some people are clearer or more awake than others, meaning they are less confused, less caught up in deluded ideas, less mesmerized by the movie of waking life, more grounded in the simplicity of nonconceptual presence. But there is no perfect person, unless by perfection we simply mean everything just as it is.

Even if some kind of sudden, enormous, apparently lasting transformation does seem to happen for a few rare people, it certainly doesn't happen for everyone, and it doesn't *need* to happen for anyone, and in fact, there is actually *no one* to whom *any* of this is happening—there is only this undivided totality that includes everything and everyone. What these words like "liberation," "awakening" or "enlightenment" actually point to is the *seeing through* of ownership and the realization of what is ever-present, undivided, uncontained and all-inclusive.

No one in the movie of waking life is without emotional and psychological weather. Some people have more or less stormy weather than others, and infinite causes and conditions (genetics, hormones, neurochemistry, nature and nurture) bring about the weather-system in any particular bodymind. The amount and intensity of the storms may have little or nothing to do with so-called awakening or lack of it.

Over the course of a lifetime, some of our neurosis may fall away and some may not. Some neurotic patterns may repeat less frequently, or with less severity, or for shorter duration when they happen, but anything is possible. In some cases, these patterns may even get worse or may return unexpectedly after a long absence, perhaps because of a shift in hormones or neurochemistry or because of a tumor in the brain or some other medical condition that may never even be discovered.

The more clarity there is, the more obvious it becomes that none of this is personal, and therefore, it no longer matters in the same way whether neurotic conditioning shows up or falls away. There may still be a natural desire to heal or clarify, to do our best and not to bring harm to ourself or to others, but when it is clear that no one is in control of what happens, then *whatever* happens is no longer a source of guilt, shame, blame or pride. There is no need to defend one's self-image or to be a supposedly enlightened "somebody" who never makes mistakes.

There is a widespread tendency to idealize spiritual teachers and put them up on pedestals, especially dead gurus. And many living teachers are only too happy to accept these projections and pretend to themselves and everyone else that they are beyond all forms of human error, uncertainty, confusion or unhappiness. But whenever teachers start insisting they never make mistakes or get upset anymore, or that anything scandalous they do is some form of "crazy wisdom" that they are doing for your benefit, hide your wallet. It's completely possible to be fully enlightened in one moment and totally deluded in the next. In fact, that fluctuation is the very nature of life.

I can tell many "awakening stories" about what has shifted in my life, what has fallen away or been clarified, but these stories all require memory and imagination to conjure up and construct. However relatively true they may be, they are always fictions. Whether the stories are about me or you or Ramana Maharshi, the person at the center of the story is no more solid or substantial than a wave in the ocean. And in the end, the greatest shift is the realization that *all* shifting is simply the impersonal play of the ever-present, all-inclusive ocean.

The thinking mind loves to rank and compare, and you'll hear some people insist that their teaching, or the teaching they identify with, is the highest, most advanced, most profound, most radical teaching of all. There are those who claim to have reached a stage of enlightenment that surpasses anything previously known to humankind. If such talk sounds suspiciously egotistical, dualistic and reminiscent of the most competitive aspects of society-at-large, it may be because it is.

That's not to say that every teacher is equally clear, or that all paths are identical or that they all lead to exactly the same place, nor is it to deny the relative reality of evolutionary development. But I'm always wary of those who claim to have risen to a level never before reached by anyone else. The clearest teachers I've met are the most ordinary. They have humility, not grandiosity. They don't claim to possess something that the rest of us do not possess. They empower those who come to them to be their own best teachers rather than encouraging dependency or the tendency to idealize authority figures and put them up on pedestals. The best teachers throw you back on yourself.

And even the best teachers make mistakes. We are all human. Hopefully, a good teacher will recognize their mistakes and won't stay confused for very long. They know where Truth resides. They're not seeking it "out there" anymore. But that doesn't mean they aren't still learning or that they "know it all."

Recognizing that a teacher is human doesn't mean that everyone is equally awake or should have equal responsibility and authority in every situation. It simply means that no wave is closer to the water than any other wave, that no "teacher" and no "student" actually exist except as momentary activities like the pedestrian walking.

Enlightenment is a word. People use this word in different ways. But as far as I'm concerned, what it points to is not a personal possession or a spiritual academy award. It's not a finish-line that you cross or a state you reside in "forever after."

Liberation doesn't mean having The Answer. It doesn't mean that we've figured out how the universe works, but rather, that the itching *need* to figure it all out dissolves. The bubble of separation and encapsulation pops and there is simply this inexplicable happening, just as it is. There is no one apart from it trying to figure it out, control it, fix it, or get something from it. There is simply *what is, as it is*. This is not an achievement. It is the recognition of what has always been so.

The most deeply enlightened figures in Zen are often portrayed as carefree fools holding on to nothing at all. They see clearly that there is nothing to grasp and no one to grasp it.

Many Ways Home

Everything happens by itself, quite spontaneously....
When effort is needed, effort will appear. When
effortlessness becomes essential, it will assert itself.

—Nisargadatta Maharaj

In emptiness, nothing collides with anything.

—Toni Packer

At the bottom-line, all of this nondual teaching has *something* to do with liberation. Maybe we could say that liberation is the end of *seeking* liberation somewhere else or imagining that liberation looks different in *any* way from right here, right now. The ultimate liberation is the falling away of the whole idea of liberation!

Some teachings undercut all of our attempts to get somewhere, to improve, to make something out of nothing. They offer a description of reality, but never a prescription for how to improve it. They don't allow any wiggle room to move away from the bottom-line truth that *this is it,* right here, right now. The beauty and the efficacy of these radical expressions lies *precisely* in their utter refusal to compromise the bottom-line truth in any way whatsoever. They don't offer any way out or anything to do. They are 100% useless. They defeat every attempt to get somewhere or to control life. These teachings hammer away relentlessly at the illusory nature of the mirage-like "me" who seems to lack something and who could seemingly *choose* to meditate or to wake up. Sometimes this uncompromisingly absolute and radical message hits the target and pops the bubble of imaginary encapsulation, and sometimes it just leaves people feeling confused and bewildered, and either way, it's *all* the divine expression, just as it is. There is no way out and no way in.

Other teachings recognize the nondual absolute but also give importance to discerning the relative difference between clarity and confusion. These teachings offer practices, contemplations, explorations, inquiries, methods, rituals, and so on for exposing the false as false and waking up to our True Nature. Sometimes this is helpful, and sometimes it just reinforces the notion that "this isn't it" and gets people more and more caught up in trying to improve and then beating themselves up when they can't seem to do it right.

Some teachings offer what I like to call the "zooming in" approach to awakening, while others go for the "zooming out" approach. The "zooming in" approach encourages you to pay careful attention to the forms of everyday life—washing the dishes, sweeping the floor, drinking tea, breathing in, breathing out. They might even recommend that you go deeply *into* sensations with awareness or that you work *with* the body through some form of yoga, breath-work, or somatic or sensory awareness work. The "zooming out" approach *seems* to go in exactly the opposite direction. They direct your attention to what is prior to everything perceivable and conceivable. They might tell you that the whole movie of waking life and all of consciousness is nothing more than a dream. They might instruct you to focus not on forms, but on the space around the forms, or they might tell you to *be* the awareness that is beholding everything. They might invite you to wonder what is aware of being aware, and then what is aware of that, until everything perceivable and conceivable is erased and all that remains is the unlocatable Ultimate Subject, the groundless ground that is prior to everything, the secret hidden in deep, deep sleep.

Who has it right? The uncompromising "this is it" people or the practice-oriented "be here now" folks? The "zooming in" people or the "zooming out" people?

In my experience, having tried all of these different approaches, I find that in the end they are all pointing to the same placeless place, the same groundlessness, the same dissolution of any imaginary separation and any imaginary problem. They just go about realizing this in different ways. Each way has different strengths and different potential pitfalls. There is no "right" way. We can argue over the seemingly contradictory models and formulations, but in the *actuality* to which they all point, no argument and no confusion remain.

Zoom in close enough, go deeply into any sensation or any form, and you'll come to the same formlessness, the same emptiness that you discover if you zoom out beyond the beyond into the vastness beyond everything known. Follow a true path all the way to the (unending) end and you'll be right here in the same placeless place that radical nonduality points out is ever-present and inescapable.

For some people, being a Zen monk is the perfect expression. For others, drinking beer and calling meditation hogwash is the perfect expression. Some teachers will tell you to sweep the floor mindfully, and others will tell you that your mindful sweeping is only a dream. Life is wonderfully playful and diverse. We aren't going to find the One True Way or the One Perfect Expression that is true for everybody all the time, unless the Way we find is no way at all—otherwise known as the Totality that includes absolutely everything—and *that* we cannot find for it is all there is.

The best teachers are like the Zen Master who hands you a candle to light your way home and then blows it out. They destroy your fixations and pull every rug out from under you. When you reach for a life preserver to keep from drowning, they kick it away from you. They don't give you false hope or stroke your ego. They don't make themselves into anything special. They throw you back on your own resources, on the simplicity of bare being. They wake you up to the reality that there is nowhere else to go, that there is no further, that this is it.

I love many diverse expressions of nonduality. And while I can certainly find significant differences between one school of Buddhism and another, or between Buddhism and Advaita, or between this teacher and that teacher, they each in their own unique way point to the same placeless place where everything dissolves.

The mind loves to focus on how this teaching compares to that teaching. It loves all the gossip about what this teacher thinks about that teacher. It loves to try to figure out who is more or less awake than someone else. But right here, right now—what are we actually talking about?

The Simplicity of What Is

In any moment, there is simply this present happening. Sometimes there are thoughts and mental movies. Sometimes they seem believable and sometimes they don't. Sometimes the sky is clear and sometimes it is cloudy. Sometimes there is a sense of being a separate person, defending a position, fighting for survival. Sometimes there is only the open, undivided, boundlessness of awareness with no center and no need to defend or oppose anything.

Sometimes the rope looks like a snake. The movie of waking life seems real. We tremble in fear, lash out in rage, weep in despair and run after the mirage lake in the desert sands to quench our thirst. And then we wake up. The movie ends. Everything that apparently happened was imaginary.

The pathless path (otherwise known as life) can seem at times like a long, hard slog. In the movie, there are barren stretches, murky stretches, heartbreaking moments, times of darkness. In many respects, life is just plain hard much of the time. But the secret of awakening is that whenever we wake up, which only happens now, all of this vanishes into thin air like the landscape of a dream. All that remains is the sound of traffic, the sensations of breathing, the twittering of a bird, the exquisite no-*thing*-ness of this moment, brimming with life, utterly complete and perfect just as it is.

Here / Now is the Beloved that we long for. We are attracted to the Beloved, drawn to the Beloved, and this attraction, this longing actually comes from our own Heart, our own True Nature, but we don't realize this at first. We search for the Beloved "out there" in many different forms—in an intimate relationship, a teacher, a guru, an enlightenment experience. And finally, in a moment of awakening, we pass through the gateless gate. We realize the Beloved is Here / Now, and in love, we find there is no separation, that the Beloved is all there is, the emptiness bursting forth as clouds and trees and pencil sharpeners and thunderstorms and light bulbs and concentration camps and meditation centers and words on a computer screen.

Here / Now is formless, and yet it is appearing as every form. It is invisible, and yet it is visible everywhere. It is as subtle as space, and yet it is more solid than the ground beneath your feet. No word can capture it, and yet, every word is only it. It's not a *particular* experience or state of consciousness, it's not an object or a substance that can be seen or grasped, it's not a conceptual formulation, it's not some mystical essence or transcendent reality apart from the messiness of ordinary everyday life. *It is just this, exactly as it is.*

When we are awake, our whole spiritual journey loses its seriousness. It melts away like a cloud formation. No one was actually running from a tiger, and no one was actually saved from this danger. The whole problem never really existed. It was only a dream.

To realize this is to be totally intimate with the world *as it actually is* (and not as we *think* it is), open to everything, holding on to nothing.

Whenever I feel discouraged or find myself overcome by a sense of despair and hopelessness, whenever I notice that I am boiling with self-righteous anger over some injustice or cruelty in the world or that I am running away from what scares me, scrambling around trying to fill the hole of emptiness and doubt with some comforting belief, it is an invitation to notice that thought has once again materialized the mirage-like "me" and overlaid the simplicity of Here / Now with some kind of story, some kind of imaginary problem. I've noticed that any attempt to resist what is happening or to seek something better only amplifies the sense of dissatisfaction. Any belief I pick up to provide meaning and comfort soon begins to seem doubtful. And yet, when *everything* that can be doubted falls away, all doubt vanishes. When resistance and seeking end, the problem vanishes. I vanish. There is simply this present moment, as it is.

Eventually, there is a growing trust in the simplicity of what is. We begin to see that whatever happens is simply another shape that life is taking, another cloud formation floating through the sky. And we realize that every moment is complete in itself, that this is enough, that nothing more or different is needed.

True freedom is the willingness for life to be as it is, no matter how it appears. This willingness is expressed in the Abrahamic religions as "Thy will be done." Paradoxically, in completely accepting everything just as it is, there is space for something truly new and creative to enter the picture. And this space is never not here.

The wonder of life, that which is sacred, the love that is at the core of every lover and beloved, *that* is equally present in every form. What is it? We can call it pure awareness, emptiness, God, the Tao—but as soon as we name it, it tends to form in the mind as *something*. And that is the most basic form of idolatry. When you stop looking for *something*, you discover the openness and the immediacy of *what is*.

Being here now is a description of reality, not a prescription to follow in order to arrive somewhere else. The Holy Reality is already here, fully complete. And if you think otherwise, then simply stop, look and listen.

Just When You Get It, It's Over!

There is no happy end. That's the beauty of it.

—Karl Renz

I guess I could be pretty pissed off about what
happened to me, but it's hard to stay mad, when
there's so much beauty in the world. Sometimes I
feel like I'm seeing it all at once, and it's too much,
my heart fills up like a balloon that's about to burst.
And then I remember to relax, and stop trying to
hold on to it, and then it flows through me like rain
and I can't feel anything but gratitude for every
single moment of my stupid little life.

—Lester (voiceover), after being shot in the head in the
movie *American Beauty*, screenplay by Alan Ball

What the greatest Zen master or Advaita sage realized
and embodied is not other than this inconceivable present happening that is ever-changing and always complete. Liberation is so simple, so effortless, so completely
available, so absolutely free. It is not the freedom to do
whatever we want or to become who we think we should
be or to make everyone else the way we want them to be.
It is rather the freedom to simply be what we are.

That, I discover again and again, is the biggest relief,

that there is nowhere to go and nothing to become.

There is simply this present happening, the boundless unicity that includes absolutely everything and that holds on to nothing. Sometimes it seems that we can recognize or allow this simplicity of being, and sometimes it seems that we can't. In times of stress, old habits tend to return and take over. We jump back onto our imaginary treadmill of suffering. The dream of separation and lack seems believable. We chase the carrot. It happens. But *all* of this is the movement of life, vanishing instant by instant into thin air. It's not personal. And in the end, in waking up or in deep sleep or at the moment of death, we see that nothing has ever really happened.

The mind loves to create idealized pictures of How Life Should Be and How I Should Be, and reality has a wonderful way of defeating all our ideas.

The more we're able to simply relax and be open to life being *exactly* the way it is, the more available this unconditional love becomes. And when it's not available, then it's not. Flowers open and close. The sky clears and then clouds up again. Some places have more stormy weather and more cloudy days than other places. This is the nature of life. Waking up to the unblemished simplicity of *what is* isn't something that happens once and then it's done. There is no end and no beginning to this infinite Self-realization, and sometimes it hurts like hell.

Years ago, I was at a concert with a popular folk-singer. He was leading the audience in singing a round, and we were finally beginning to learn the words and get the feel of it, and then it ended. "Life is like a song," the folk-singer joked. "Just when you start to get the hang of it, it's over." That's not bad news. That's just the way it is. Everything plays its part and then it dies and becomes food for something else in an endless recycling where nothing is wasted and nothing is ever really lost. In that sense, we can't ever really waste our time, lose our lives, or miss the boat. Wherever we go, here we are. Even the apparent mistakes are all part of the process, the grit that creates the pearl.

During the last year she was alive, at age 95, my mother said many times, "It's so freeing to realize that nothing really matters." She said it joyously, with relief, as if a burden had been lifted. She also said over and over, "Love yourself."

Love sees the True Self, the boundless absolute, right here in the messiness and imperfection of this human life. Love sees that nothing matters in the way we habitually *think* it does, and at the same time, it recognizes *every-thing* as the Holy Reality.

In the end, it gets simpler and simpler. Watching the clouds, hearing the birds sing, drinking a cup of coffee, breathing in and breathing out, biting the fingers, wiggling the toes, opening the heart, *being* Here / Now – *this* that you cannot not be – nothing is more important than just this.

Acknowledgments

Special thanks to D Allen for the question that set this book in motion. Thank you to D Allen, Colleen Loehr and Nathan Gill for your invaluable feedback on this manuscript and for your friendship. Many other teachers, gurus, colleagues and friends have helped to illuminate the pathless path from Here to Here over the years, some are quoted in this book (some are not), and I thank you all. Last but not least, a very warm thank you to Julian and Catherine Noyce for publishing my books.

CONSCIOUS.TV is a TV channel which broadcasts on the internet at www.conscious.tv. It also has programmes shown on several satellite and cable channels around the world. The channel aims to stimulate debate, question, enquire, inform, enlighten, encourage and inspire people in the areas of Consciousness, Non-Duality and Science. It also has a section called 'Life Stories' with many fascinating interviews.

There are over 200 interviews to watch including several with communicators on Non-Duality including Jeff Foster, Steve Ford, Suzanne Foxton, Gangaji, Greg Goode, Scott Kiloby, Richard Lang, Francis Lucille, Roger Linden, Wayne Liquorman, Jac O'Keefe, Mooji, Catherine Noyce, Tony Parsons, Satyananda, Richard Sylvester, Rupert Spira, Florian Schlosser, Mandi Solk and Pamela Wilson. There is also an interview with UK Krishnamurti.

Do check out the channel as we are interested in your feedback and any ideas you may have for future programmes. Email us at info@conscious.tv with your ideas or if you would like to be on our email newsletter list.

CONSCIOUS.TV and NON-DUALITY PRESS
present two unique DVD releases

CONVERSATIONS ON NON-DUALITY – VOLUME 1
Tony Parsons – The Open Secret • Rupert Spira –
The Transparency of Things – Parts 1 & 2 • Richard
Lang – Seeing Who You Really Are

CONVERSATIONS ON NON-DUALITY – VOLUME 2
Jeff Foster – Life Without a Centre • Richard
Sylvester – I Hope You Die Soon • Roger Linden –
The Elusive Obvious

Available to order from: www.non-dualitypress.org

New Book now available to order from Non-Duality Press

Conversations on Non-Duality
Twenty-Six Awakenings

The book explores the nature of true happiness,

awakening, enlightenment and the 'Self' to be realised. It features 26 expressions of liberation, each shaped by different life experiences and offering a unique perspective.

The collection explores the different ways 'liberation' happened and 'suffering' ended. Some started with therapy, self-help workshops or read books written by spiritual masters, while others travelled to exotic places and studied with gurus. Others leapt from the despair of addiction to drugs and alcohol to simply waking up unexpectedly to a new reality.

The 26 interviews included in the book are with: David Bingham, Daniel Brown, Sundance Burke, Katie Davis, Peter Fenner, Steve Ford, Jeff Foster, Suzanne Foxton, Gagaji, Richard Lang, Roger Linden, Wayne Liquorman, Francis Lucille, Mooji, Catherine Noyce, Jac O'Keeffe, Tony Parsons, Bernie Prior, Halina Pytlasinska, Genpo Roshi, Florian Schlosser, Mandi Solk, Rupert Spira, James Swartz, Richard Sylvester and Pamela Wilson.

CPSIA information can be obtained
at www.ICGtesting.com
Printed in the USA
FSOW02n0021131015
12107FS